Acoustic Guitar Styles

Acoustic Guitar Styles

Larry Sandberg

Routledge
New York and London

Published in 2002 by
Routledge
29 West 35th Street
New York, NY 10001

Published in Great Britain by
Routledge
11 New Fetter Lane
London EC4P 4EE

Routledge is an imprint of the Taylor & Francis Group.

Printed on acid-free, 250-year-life paper.
Manufactured in the United States of America.

10   9   8   7   6   5   4   3   2   1

Library of Congress Cataloging-in-Publication Data

Sandberg, Larry.
    Acoustic guitar styles/Larry Sandberg.
    p. cm.
    ISBN 0-415-93727-2
    1. Guitar—Instruction and study. I. Title.

MT580.S32   2002
784.87′193—dc21   2001040814

Contents

Introduction

I've written this book for guitarists interested in developing solo techniques in American-roots guitar styles. Early country music (often called old-time music), bluegrass, and blues are the basis of most of present-day America's popular guitar styles and, in fact, of much guitar music throughout the world. Contemporary guitarists who are familiar with roots styles generally make better, more versatile, and sometimes even more creative musicians than those who have no such history in their playing. Learning how to play the styles in this book also qualifies you, and adds to your depth, for working in every style of modern American popular music.

How you get this history into your playing is important. For the most part, American-roots music is rhythm music, often based on dance forms. At the very least, it's foot-tapping music. Techniques for playing this kind of music arise out of physical gestures that are intimately concerned with timekeeping. Strumming the guitar, sawing the fiddle, banging out "clawhammer" beats on the banjo, and even squeezing a squeezebox in and out are all rhythmic gestures that help keep time.

Many guitarists who learn traditional music nowadays approach this music in terms of set pieces to be memorized, without working from the rhythmic basis of the strumming and picking patterns that produce the music. Learning rote pieces note by note makes it hard to get the rhythmic feeling. The set-piece approach also encourages copying them to the exclusion of creativity. Some players manage to transcend the disempowering limitations of this approach anyway. Most, in my experience, don't, and with unhappy results. At a certain point, they wonder why their music has gone dead. It's because it was never alive in the first place.

This book keeps the music alive by requiring your active participation. Unlike most other guitar books, it doesn't teach you lots of new songs or use new material to introduce new techniques. Rather, it relies on a small basic repertoire of songs, asking you to play them in different ways, in different styles, in different keys, and with different feelings. It also poses choices and asks you to make your own decisions. In short, it asks you to do what real musicians do. At best, you'll learn to be a creator. But even if you do go to a repertoire book or a teacher to learn a piece by rote, you'll be able to see better just what that process was that led that piece's creator to create it.

Some teachers think that learning to make your own decisions is "advanced," but my experience has been heartbreakingly the opposite. If students don't see decision making and problem solving as part of the learning process from the outset, they're not going to get into a problem-solving mind-set later on. There's only one hitch: you have to have some degree of musical talent to take advantage of this approach. In the nature of things, many guitar instruction books are written for people who have little or no talent, because a great many people don't. This book does not make that assumption, so it's not for everyone.

Therefore, this book is short on rote and long, I hope, on engagement. It shows you how to solve problems on your own by showing you solutions in principle rather than by rote. It doesn't, as the old proverb goes, give you a fish. It teaches you to fish for yourself. But you have to learn to bait your own hook. It's hard work, much harder than just doing what somebody tells you to do and then moving on to the next set of orders. It's also more fun. But be prepared. Some of the "creative-work" assignments could take hours, days, or weeks of experimenting on your own to master.

This is not a book for the absolute beginner. I'm assuming that you've had at least several weeks of basic training. I begin at a pretty basic level, in any case. But I'm assuming that you've at least learned some chord shapes, know that the first (highest) string is the one closest to the floor, and understand chord diagrams. I'm also assuming that you can strum through a few songs and either can follow music notation or tablature or have a good enough ear to work exclusively by listening to the CD selections. (Most people need the notes or tabs to help out their ears.) I start off with a review of basics in part I and then get into a steeper learning curve in part II.

Acknowledgments

Thanks to . . .

My own teachers of roots guitar styles, Happy Traum and Dick Weissman, who taught me to teach as well as to play.

All my students over the years, especially those at Swallow Hill Music Association and the Denver Folklore Center.

Mary Flower, for singing several of the vocal selections on the CD.

Harry Tuft of the Denver Folklore Center, an inspiration for keeping roots music alive.

Sam Burns, Jeff Jaros, and the gang down at the Denver Folklore Center for helping me waltz when I was stuck in the two-step.

Scott Smith, for recording the CD selections at the Sawtelle Studio of the Swallow Hill Music Association.

Editor Richard Carlin, for suggesting and commissioning this book, and his colleagues at Routledge: Robert Byrne, Julie Ho; and copyeditor Ann Edahl.

Preliminaries

How to Use This Book

Basics

The first part of this book is designed to establish a basic set of chord-changing skills that you absolutely must have in order to make the most out of the later section. It's not hard, but you must be comfortable with these basic chord shapes and changes before proceeding. This book is about rhythm. It's about learning a variety of beats and rhythmic feelings in your picking hand. And if you can't make your chord changes on time, you're not going to be able to keep a steady beat.

Notes and Tablature

Tablature is a dangerous friend: two-faced, fickle, and flattering. There's something about tablature that's like painting by numbers. It discourages thinking.

Reading notes is a little better because it seems to engage the mind in a more exciting way. But it can also be dangerous because it still puts you in the mind-set of doing what you're told, rather than figuring things out for yourself.

Learning by ear is good because it trains the ear and encourages experiment. The only way to see whether something works is to put your finger down somewhere and see if it's the right note. If it's not, try again. The great virtue of this approach is that it teaches you that when you play a wrong note through experimentation, it's part of a process rather than a mistake. This is the single most important lesson you have to learn in order to be a creative musician.

Learning by ear and by experiment are also more demanding than learning by rote. Being your own person is always harder than following orders. Living in a protected environment completely shielded from problems doesn't teach you how to solve them. You wouldn't raise your child this way, so why would I want to teach you to play this way? Instead, I set you up with problems that you're likely to succeed at to help you succeed in other instances. Sometimes you've got training wheels. Sometimes you're on your own. The problem-solving and experimental "creative-work" tasks are easy at first, getting harder as you progress through the book.

This book combines all of the approaches I've outlined. It uses notes and tablature because it has to; books are a written medium. It uses a CD to encourage ear training and provide aural examples. And it assigns creative exercises to make you think things out on your own and experiment. Be fearless. Don't be afraid of making mistakes. You will play wrong notes. You should play wrong notes. How else are you going to learn where the right ones are?

Setting Your Pace

The second part of this book consists of sections devoted to particular styles. Each section develops a series of techniques progressively and cumulatively. In almost every case, it's important to master a given technique at least to a level of basic comfort and assured rhythmic flow before you proceed to the next. From time to time, I give you some advice, based on experience with lots of students. Be sure to stop here and work on this, I say. Or, it's okay to go on, I say, to the next section while you're still working on this technique. But as much as I try to give the feeling that I'm there working with you, I'm just not. You have to be your own judge of how fast to take things. Be conservative. You can't be too conservative.

Some of the "creative work" I throw out at you is just there to hone your skills. Other assignments require a lot of thought and trial and error, possibly involving weeks of experiment as a cumulative, ongoing process. It's okay to keep working on these while you move on to a following section. You'll have to figure out your own learning style. Just remember that progress does not get made overnight in music. It comes from doing the same thing over and over and over until you get it right. That might be a dozen times for one person or a thousand for another—whatever it takes.

Finding Your Place and Using the CD

Although this book is divided into chapters, the real units of thought are sections called *tracks*. Each track section in the book refers to a corresponding track number on the accompanying CD.

The CD has many short tracks, adding up to as much music as a CD can hold. I suggest you set your CD player to its *repeat track* setting when you study a track, so that you can play the same track over and over again. This is what real musicians do when they study a piece of music. Like learning to move your fingers, learning by ear requires more repetition than beginners or nonmusicians believe.

Listening

The best way to learn the music in this book is with the active support and surrounding of a living musical culture. Second best is to immerse yourself in CD listening. Broad listening is good, but, for purposes of learning, a small collection for intense and repeated listening is even better.

This book makes frequent listening suggestions. There's nothing esoteric about most of the names listed. They're all well known traditional artists, most of whom have served as models for contemporary guitarists for many years. Check out the online or in-store retail CD databases, and you'll see many recordings by most of these artists. You can even listen online to streaming audio of many selections. And good big-city or academic libraries, or small libraries with interlibrary loan service, are liable to have recordings of their work. Bear in mind that classic recordings of traditional music often go in and out of print, reappearing at times with album different titles on different labels. Therefore, search by song title and artist in the CD databases.

Also look for different artists' versions of the same song. Listening to different versions teaches you about the way personal styles develop and about the degree of latitude you have in making up your own arrangements.

One of the big differences between successful guitarists and wannabes (to use a brutal but perfectly truthful term) is in the quality and intensity of listening study. Listening ranks in importance along with practice itself.

Tuning

Track 1 on the CD sounds out the high and low E strings as a tuning reference.

Basic Chord Shapes

The chord diagram chart in figure 2.1 gives the basic chord shapes you need to know to play the music in this book. I'll add a few more later on. Pay careful attention to the fingerings. When you first learn to strum, you have some latitude to choose among alternative chord fingerings. When you start to add extra notes to chords in order to play melodies—as you will do in part II—only certain fingerings work. Make sure that you use the fingerings shown in these chord diagrams—especially for the F and G chords. For the A chord, on the other hand, use whatever works.

    T = thumb
    1 = index
    2 = middle
    3 = ring
    4 = pinky

Some books, and most classical guitar music, use *P* (from Spanish, *pulgar*) to indicate the thumb. If you've had piano training, you'll have to get out of the habit of using 12345 where the guitar uses T1234.

Along with the chord name, you'll notice one or several pairs of numbers above each chord diagram. The first of these numbers refers to the bass (low) string that in most circumstances most strongly supports the sound of each chord. The second number refers to an alternate possibility. You'll learn how to use these bass notes starting with track 5 and alternating bass notes starting with track 10. No need to worry about them yet.

FIGURE 2.1. BASIC GUITAR CHORDS, FINGERINGS, AND BASS NOTES

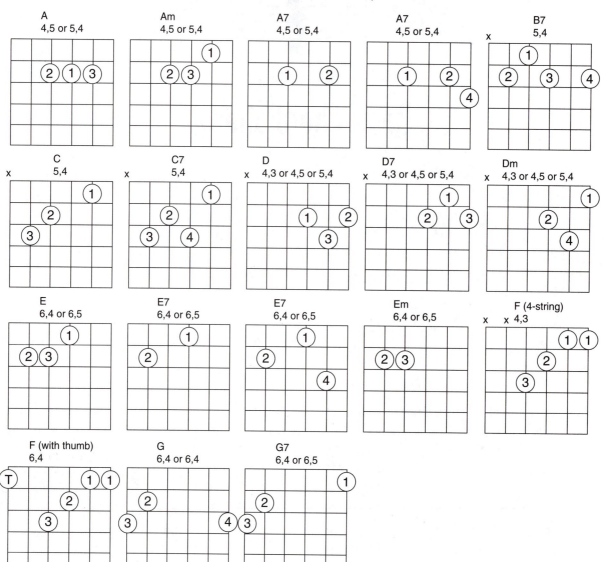

Chord-Progression Practice

Chord Progressions

When you sing a song or play it on an instrument such as a flute or trumpet, you produce a melody that consists of only one note at a time. In our culture, we usually accompany the melody with simultaneous groups of other notes that sound good to us when they're played along. This process is called *harmony.* The groups of notes are called *chords.*

Songs gain interest when they have melodies that require more than one chord. Hardly any songs in our culture have only one chord; we find them too boring. (Some other cultures have more interesting rhythmic or other values in their music than ours does, so that one-chord songs may be more common. But in our culture, harmony assumes a greater value.) A relatively small number of simple songs, especially nursery rhymes like "Skip to My Lou" and "Mary Had a Little Lamb," have only two chords. In roots music and most of today's popular music, three or four chords seems about right.

Musicians call the order of the chords used in a given song the *chord progression* or *chord changes* (or just *progression* or *changes*). Practicing chord progressions is a good way to get your fingers working. That way you can concentrate on your moves without worrying about an actual song. Then, once the progressions are in your fingers, it's easier to gain control of the song as a structure, with words, and chord changes coming in the right places in relation to the words, and sung melodies, and so on. In music, it's good to break down every bit of the learning process into component parts and assimilate them one at a time. People who succeed best in music are generally people who naturally have this learning skill. I've arranged this book along this principle and will help you with it the best I can. Following this principle, the best way to learn chord changes is to focus on the changes alone, without worrying about the words or melodies of the songs they belong to.

The chord-progression exercises that follow prepare you to play all the music in this book and more. If you're teaching yourself from this book, you may also want to obtain a songbook of well-known songs and review actual songs that use these chords. If you're a teacher, you may want to supplement this section by offering your students additional songs from a songbook or handouts.

Making Chord Changes

You've *got* to be on top of making clean, quick, and efficient chord changes in order to make your music flow. It's in the very nature of learning the guitar to think that the fretting hand comes first. (Like most guitar authors, I'll refer to the fretting hand as the left hand and the picking hand as the right hand, even while knowing that some lefties choose to play the opposite way.) Unfortunately, putting the left hand first is a wrong-headed way to approach rhythm music, or possibly any music. The right hand must come first. The right hand places the notes in time and determines the pulse and flow of the music. If you play a wrong note, it's only a wrong note. Wrong notes come and then are gone. If you play out of time, you alter the flow of the music, and it persists eternally. You've destroyed the music to its core.

It's not my purpose in this book to teach you how to make every chord change efficiently. It can't really be the purpose of any book; the proper medium for this kind of in-depth study of finger mechanics is personal instruction or, second best, video. And there aren't even clear-cut right ways to teach changes because different things work for different people.

But let me give you a few philosophical and mechanical hints that may help you if you're having trouble making clean chord changes.

1. **Make sure you practice enough.** Many people who approach the guitar without a prior musical background just don't understand how much repetition is required to learn an instrument.

2. **Practice smart.** Mere repetition won't help you if you're repeating the same sloppy move. In fact, it will harm you because you're practicing making that sloppy move, and all that will happen is that you'll get good at making a sloppy move. Using some of the principles in the rest of this list, think out the chord change better and experiment to get it right.

3. **Use your wrist.** The angle at which you hold your wrist positions your hand in order to let the fingers do their job best. Sometimes a chord change that's hard to make neatly when you think fingers alone becomes easy if you just move your wrist around. For example, almost everyone senses that the best way to get from E to B7 is to twist around the angle of your hand, pivoting on the second finger (fifth string) and using the wrist to bring the remaining fingers into the position they need to be. This kind of thinking applies to other changes too.

Also remember that your wrist is in turn connected to the rest of your body. Some chord changes involve moving your elbow; some you can feel all the way up to your armpit. And almost any move of the wrist will also require you to move your thumb. Don't get dependent on keeping your thumb rooted in one spot. It needs to move around.

   4. **Keep your fingers close to the fingerboard.** Don't let them splay out during chord changes. A good example of this is going from Am to E because the shapes of these two chords are the same. Absolutely don't let that shape fall apart when you make the chord change; instead, move the entire shape as a unit from strings 2,3,4 to strings 3,4,5.

   Now apply this principle to the chord change C to G7 and also think *wrist* while you do it. Instead of relocating each finger one at a time, use your wrist to rotate the C shape, *as a unit,* into the G7 shape. Got the idea?

   5. **To some extent, you can apply the thinking of paragraph 4 to almost every chord change.** Look for similarities between chord shapes and try to find *guide fingers* to help navigate those changes whenever you can. Going from D to a two-finger A7, move your first and second fingers as a unit from strings 1,3 to strings 2,4.

   How about D to E? You may feel comfortable sliding your index finger down the third string from the second to the first fret, not even leaving the string, and building the rest of the chord change around this guide finger move. Or you may prefer to concentrate on your second finger, moving it vertically (without leaving the area of the second fret) from the first to the fifth string, and build your chord change around that move. I'm not sure either of these moves is necessarily better than the other. What's important is that in both cases a neat gesture underlies the chord change and organizes the fingers.

Practicing Chord Progressions

Following are some chord progressions to play and practice. Get them into your fingers so that when you start working with the right hand later on in the book, you'll already have your left hand under control. If you're already absolutely secure about making these chord changes, you can skip them. If you happen to already know some strumming or picking patterns, feel free to use them. Otherwise, just keep a steady pulse by brushing down with your thumb or a flat pick.

Track 2: G Am C D

In track 2, I've recorded a good way to practice chord changes when your fingers are having a tough time. First, do what you can't hear on the track: analyze the chord change according to the principles discussed in the previous section and figure out what you need to do with your fingers (and wrist and arm) to make the change more efficient.

   Then learn how to make the change evenly. Evenness is the most important quality you can cultivate. You get good at what you practice, so if you practice making chord changes unevenly, you'll get good at playing unevenly. Strive to keep your chord changes even by not playing them at a faster tempo than your fingers can manage.

   Track 2 demonstrates a good way to give your fingers enough time to make chord changes evenly. The picking is simple. I'm just brushing down across the strings with my thumb. You could also be brushing down with a flat pick if you want. Foot tap a slow, even four beats, counting *one-two-three-four,* and make it your business to be ready with the next chord by the time you get to the next *one.* Don't necessarily keep the chord fingers down for all three beats between the *ones,* but use the time to make the chord change. Then, still going slowly, reduce your count to *one-two-three,* giving yourself one less beat to make the chord change. Then down to two beats. Finally, make the chord change on every beat.

   This example uses four chords. If you're a beginner, or if you find a given chord change particularly troublesome, isolate it and practice it by going back and forth between only two chords at a time. When you practice a chord progression, don't play it just once and then stop. Keep on playing it around and around, over and over again.

Track 3: C Am Dm G7

Work with this chord progression the same way you did in track 2. This time, do one more exercise in analyzing chord-change moves.

   C to Am. Your first and second fingers play the same notes in both these chords. Don't let them leave their strings as you make the change! You may, however, want to let your second finger slide along the fourth string a little toward the nut of the guitar. Do this by releasing thumb pressure a bit, but don't let your finger actually lose contact with the string.

   Am to Dm. Keep your first and second fingers together and move them as a unit from strings 2,4 to strings 1,3. I recommend that you play the second-string note with your pinky rather than ring finger. It's harder at first because the pinky is naturally weak, but as it gains strength, it actually makes this chord shape easier because it eliminates a stretch.

   Dm to G7. Keep your index finger in place on the first string first fret and bring the rest of your fingers in place to make the low notes of the G7 by rotating your wrist counterclockwise and perhaps dropping it and angling it forward a little.

   As you continue to work with chord progressions, keep thinking about your moves this way whenever you come across a chord change that gives you trouble.

Track 4: D C G D

Songs tend to have chord progressions that are felt in units of four. This is a gross generalization, but it's true enough that it pays to practice progressions this way. It just feels natural and leads you more naturally into sensing how the chords fall in a given song. That's why I keep giving you chord progressions in units of four chords.

   Sometimes the felt unit of four involves a starting and an ending chord that are the same. As you cycle the chord progression around by playing it over and over, it's important not to lose count of the first and last chords. Cultivate a sense of where the last D ends and the first D begins again in track 4.

   Similarly, try these progressions:

   G   C   D7 G

   Am Dm E7 Am

Chord Progressions for Practice

Here are a whole bunch of chord progressions. Using the mechanical and analytical techniques you've just learned, work on them until you can play them smoothly and evenly. You've already seen a few of them.

After this chapter, you'll be working on picking and strumming patterns in the right hand. Your right hand just won't be able to keep the music flowing if it has to wait for your left hand to catch up. Even though you won't be using every one of these chord changes in this book, I can guarantee that you'll be using them later in life. So it's best to get fluent with them now.

A	D	E7	A
A	D	A	E7
A	G	D	A
Am	Dm	E7	Am
Am	Dm	Am	E7
Am	G	Em	Am
C	F	G7	C
C	F	C	G7
C	Am	Dm	G7
D	G	A7	D
D	G	D	A7
D	C	G	D
Dm	C	A7	Dm
Dm	C	Dm	A7
Dm	F	Am	Dm
E	A	B7	E
E	A	E	B7
E	D	A	E
Em	Am	B7	Em
Em	Am	Em	B7
Em	G	D	Am
G	C	D7	G
G	C	G	D7
G	F	C	G

Learning these progressions will put you in good shape for the future. We'll review some of them, and work with others, in the sections to come.

Basic Picking and Plucking Patterns

All the guitar styles in this book have one thing in common. They all depend on some alternating relationship between higher and lower notes. For practical purposes, *high* refers to notes produced on the three high strings and *low* refers to notes produced on the three low strings. The give and take between the high and low strings is the basis for the pianistic quality of much solo guitar playing, in which one guitar sounds like two—one high and one low.

Even the simplest strumming patterns make use of this principle. In this section, you'll work on splitting up bass (low) and treble (high) in this way: first, you'll pluck a bass note on one of the low strings, and then you'll brush down across the three highest strings. This picking pattern can be played either flat-pick or finger style. I suggest you try both.

With a flat pick, play both the single bass note and the treble brush as downstrokes with the pick.

With bare fingers or bare fingers plus thumb pick, play the bass note with the thumb and then brush down across the high strings with the index finger. Some people use the index plus middle and sometimes ring fingers as well. See what suits you best.

People who wear finger picks along with a thumb pick usually prefer to make both the bass note and the high brush strokes with two separate moves of the thumb. (Finger picks usually get caught in the strings if you brush down with them.)

The brush stroke generally sounds rich and full when you play all three treble strings. That's what I've written out in the music examples. Many players freely vary their brush stroke, frequently hitting only two or sometimes even one string in order to bring out certain notes within the chord. Learning how to control this process so that it's reasoned rather than random is an art in itself. The easiest thing is just to go for all three strings all the time, and most people do. But feel free to experiment.

In finger-style playing, the low strings generally belong to the thumb and high strings belong to the fingers. This "rule of thumb" gets broken a lot, even in this book, but it's a good starting point.

As far as the left hand goes, remember that this style, and every other style in this book, is completely chord-based. Always keep the fingers of the left hand on the complete chord shape. Even though the musical notation in a given spot may not show every note in the chord, you should always have the complete chord shape in place.

Track 5: Bass-Brush in C

Listen to track 5 to get the feeling for the rhythm and for the sense of alternating the bass note and the brush. You may use a barred F for the F chord if you wish, but better yet, use this opportunity to practice the F chord played with the thumb on the sixth string (see figure 2.1). You'll also notice that my choice of bass notes conforms to the first bass note suggested with each of the chord diagrams in figure 2.1.

Why am I choosing to play the bass notes I do? The answer is simple. The bass note I'm playing for each chord is its *tonic* note: the note that the chord is named after. In other words, for my bass note in the C chord, I'm playing a C note, for the F chord an F note, and for the G7 chord a G note. This choice of bass notes is the one that most firmly establishes the sound of the chord in the listener's ear. For this reason, it's the preferred choice. This is a general rule, and one that gets broken all the time. All you have to do is decide that in a given place in a song, some other bass note sounds better. But for learning purposes, the tonic note is the one you want to train yourself to use automatically.

Remember to follow the picking instructions I gave at the beginning of the chapter, and always keep down the complete chord shape. If you have any problems making the chords, rehearse the changes before you start picking. The object in practicing is to concentrate on one thing at a time. This exercise is to develop right-hand technique. In order to concentrate on that, you first need to have your left-hand work securely under control. Also remember to play this exercise over and over again, without stopping.

TRACK 5. BASS-BRUSH IN C

CREATIVE WORK. Figure out how to play this picking pattern on the following chord progressions.

C F   C F
C G7 C G7
F G7 C F
G F   C G

Track 6: Bass-Brush in A

Tracks 6 and 7 provide another two exercises to give your right hand the feeling of locating the appropriate bass string and then brushing. Try to get reasonably accurate, but don't worry too much about consistent perfection. This is one spot where you can move on without being absolutely perfect. You may also feel that this pattern is pretty boring. It is. The idea is to move on quickly to something more interesting.

TRACK 6. BASS-BRUSH IN A

CREATIVE WORK. Figure out how to play this picking pattern on the following chord progressions:

A D A   D
A E7 A E7
A G D   A
D C A7 D (same bass note for A7 as for A)
D E7 A D

Track 7: Bass-Brush in E

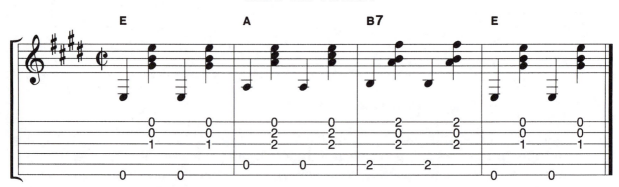

TRACK 7. BASS-BRUSH IN E

CREATIVE WORK. Figure out how to play this rhythm on the following chord progressions. Be extra careful about choosing the preferred bass notes in the last progression—they're all over the place. Your choice of bass notes for the F chord depends on which F shape you choose to play.

     E   A   E   A

     E   B7   E   B7

     E   D   A   E

     C   E7   F   G7 **(same bass note for E7 as for E)**

Track 8: Bass-Brush in D in Three-Four Time

Now let's play a different beat. In most American popular music, we feel the beat either in units of two (and multiples of two) or in units of three (and multiples of three). So far you've been playing bass-brush, a unit of two. Now let's try bass-brush-brush, a unit of three.

Music that's felt in units of three beats is called *three-quarter time* or *three-four time.* Or sometimes people just say *in three.* When a piece is in units of two, it's usually just called (depending on whether the feel of it is marchlike or smooth) regular time, standard time, *two* or *four,* or *two-four* or *four-four.* Or it's just left unsaid.

In order to get three components into your strumming pattern, simply add one more brush stroke in an even *one-two-three,* bass-brush-brush rhythm. The sound of the thumb stroke firmly establishes the feeling of *one* on the first of every three beats.

TRACK 8. BASS-BRUSH IN D IN THREE-FOUR TIME

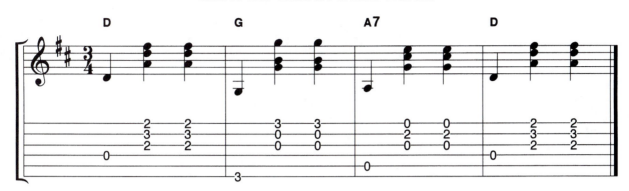

CREATIVE WORK. Figure out how to play this picking pattern on the following chord progressions:

    D G   D   G

    D A7 D   A7

    G A7 D7 G (same bass note for D7 as for D)

    D E7 A7 D

    D C   G   D

Track 9: Bass-Brush in G in Three-Four Time

TRACK 9. BASS-BRUSH IN G IN THREE-FOUR TIME

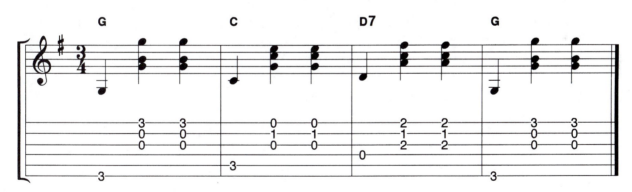

CREATIVE WORK. Figure out how to play this picking pattern on the following chord progressions. Play them first in three; then play them in standard time.

    G C   G   C

    G D7 G   D7

    G E7 A7 D7

    A7 D7 G7 C

    G A7 D7 G

Using Alternating Bass Notes
to Vary Picking and Strumming Patterns

Now we're going to get down to the central feature of American traditional guitar styles: alternating bass notes. You've noticed by now that the picking patterns used so far sound boring because of the repeated bass notes. By going back and forth between two different bass notes, you can add a huge amount of interest to your playing.

The principle is simple. The first time you hit a bass note, make it the tonic bass note for the chord. The next time you hit a bass note, pluck an adjacent string that belongs to the chord. Keep this alternation absolutely constant, with one exception. Make sure that when you start a new line of a song, always start with the tonic bass note, even if it means repeating the same note with which you ended the previous line. The music just sounds stronger when you start a phrase with the tonic note. You'll probably find yourself doing it instinctively without thinking too hard about it.

Cultivate this rule until it becomes second nature. Only then should you start breaking it. You'll be doing just that in some later examples, but not yet.

Alternating-Bass Patterns

The chord chart in chapter 2 (figure 2.1) lists the most popular alternating-bass possibilities for each chord. For your convenience, I list them again here in tabular form. I don't use all of these possibilities in this book because I have my personal favorites. For example, in my own playing, I rarely use 5,6 as alternating bass notes for the A chord. Why? I don't know. I don't care. On the other hand, my friend Mary Flower, who sings some of the songs on the accompanying CD and is a wonderful guitarist in her own right, does like to use 5,6.

You can already start making your own choices. Even at this basic level, these small differences add up to make one guitar stylist sound different from another.

Basic Chord Shape	Alternating-Bass Strings
A, Am, A7	5,4 or 5,6
B7	5,4
C, C7	5,4
D, Dm, D7	4,5 or 4,3 or 5,4*
E, Em, E7	6,4 or 6,5
4-string F	4,3
4-string F plus thumb on sixth string	6,4

*Almost every alternating-bass pattern in this table starts with a lower note and alternates to a higher one. Because this habit is so prevalent, many guitarists use the 5,4 pattern with the D chord even though the fifth string is not the tonic note. Depending on the context and on how the chord sounds against the melody, you can get away with this to greater or lesser degree depending on your taste.

LISTENING. You'll hear alternating bass playing in the work of many historically influential guitarists, usually coupled with other stylistic aspects more complex than the simple patterns you'll work on in this chapter. Give a listen to Jimmie Rodgers (available on several reissue labels), whose 1930s work established him as a founder of modern country music and whose strumming style has never been excelled for combining clarity, simplicity, and excitement. Listen to the punchy alternating bass notes with which Woody Guthrie, the troubadour of the 1940s and 1950s and a founder of the social protest song, accompanies his singing (e.g., *Dust Bowl Ballads* on the Rounder label). Doc Watson is a master of several of the styles in this book. Check out one of his solo CDs, such as *Doc Watson* (Vanguard), to hear most clearly how alternating bass notes are at the root of Doc's more complex style.

Track 10: Alternating-Bass Strumming in C

Notice how straightforward and natural sounding the alternating bass notes on this track sound and how much interest they add to strumming on chords. With this and the following examples, practice each chord separately. Then incorporate them into the entire progression. If necessary, practice the progression two chords at a time.

TRACK 10. ALTERNATING-BASS STRUMMING IN C

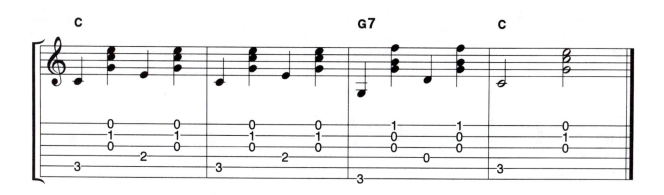

CREATIVE WORK. Use the alternating-bass pattern on the following progressions. In this and all the other exercises in the following tracks, *play each chord twice so you have space to use the alternating bass notes.*

C G7 F   C
C F   C   F
C G   C   G
C F   G7 C
G F   G   F

Track 11: Alternating-Bass Strumming in C, in Three-Four Time

Playing with alternating basses in three-four time is easy. Just use the bass-brush-brush pattern.

TRACK 11. ALTERNATING-BASS STRUMMING IN C, IN THREE-FOUR TIME

CREATIVE WORK. Strum the following chord progressions using alternating bass notes in three. Remember, play each chord for two bass notes' worth of strumming.

    F C F   C

    C G7 C G7

    C F G7 C

    G F C   G

    C G F   C

Track 12: Alternating-Bass Strumming in G

To give you a sense of how these exercises sound in real life, the CD track includes both slow and fast versions.

TRACK 12. ALTERNATING-BASS STRUMMING IN G

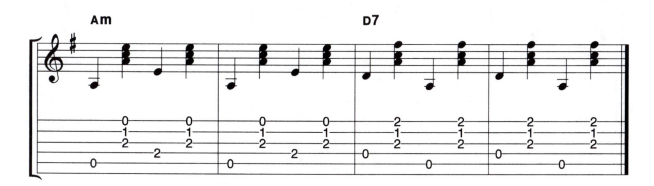

CREATIVE WORK. Strum with alternating bass notes on the following progressions. Then play them again, this time in three, using the bass-brush-brush pattern.

    G Em G Em

    G D7 G D7

    G C D7 G

    G F C   G

    Am G Am G

Track 13: Alternating-Bass Strumming in A Minor, in Three-Four Time

TRACK 13. ALTERNATING-BASS STRUMMING IN A MINOR, IN THREE-FOUR TIME

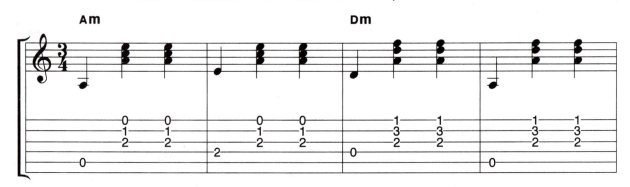

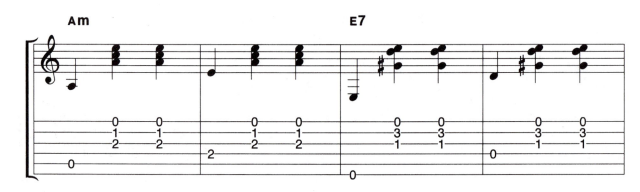

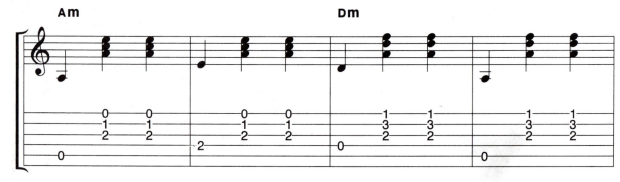

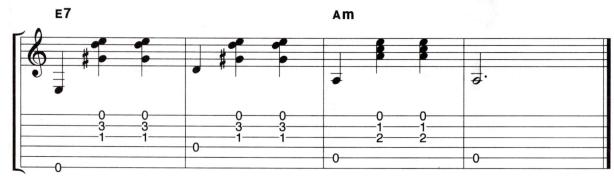

CREATIVE WORK. Play the following chord progressions with the alternating-bass pattern in three. Then play them again in standard time, using the bass-brush pattern.

Am C   E7 Am

Am G7 C   Am

Dm C   Am Dm

Dm F   E7 Am

Am B7 E7 Am

Track 14: Alternating-Bass Strumming in D

Track 14 moves along at a reasonably quick pace on the CD, what musicians call *medium tempo*. A lot of real-life music gets played at around this speed. Amateurs often play songs too fast. Never be afraid of taking it easy.

Notice how on this track I've chosen to use 5,4 as the alternating bass notes on D.

TRACK 14. ALTERNATING-BASS STRUMMING IN D

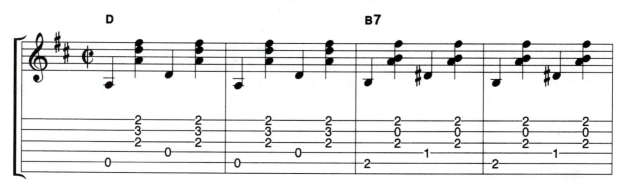

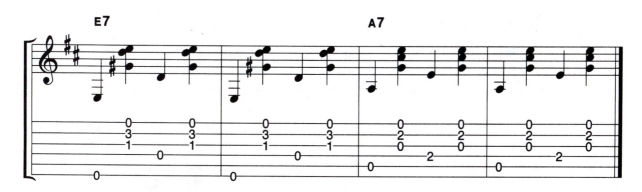

CREATIVE WORK. Apply alternating-bass strumming to the following progressions. There are three possibilities for alternating-bass patterns in D: 4,5 and 4,3 and 5,4. Try them all. Experiment with the sounds. Start deciding which you like best in which progressions, and let them become your habits.

D	G	A7	D
D	C	G	D
Am	D	Am	D
D	F	G	A
B7	E7	A7	D

MORE CREATIVE WORK. Go back and apply alternating-bass picking to all the other chord-progression exercises from chapter 3, in both two-four and three-four time. If you feel you need more chord practice, keep on working on this section before you proceed. If you feel comfortable with your chord changes, keep working on this while you're assimilating the new techniques from the next section on hammering.

Also, try making up some chord progressions of your own. In the earlier twentieth century, the basis of American popular music was the show tune, written by composers trained in European music. They often used complicated chords in complicated progressions. Two successive revolutions, those of 1950s rock and of the Beatles/Bob Dylan era, put an end to this tradition. These revolutions also introduced American roots music, rather than European light classical music, as the underlying model for popular song.

Since then, songwriters have generally relied on simple chords, often arranged in simple, stereotypical progressions like the ones we've been playing. Some—Beatles tunes come especially to mind—were created by experimenting to create strikingly unusual progressions out of simple chords. There's no reason you can't start doing this yourself. Today. Right now. Just play a couple of chords one after another. See if the combination satisfies you. Then add a third. *Hint:* Sometimes you need to add that third chord to make the first two click together.

Hammering

Track 15: Hammering on Am

I'd like to introduce one more technique before moving on to some songs. It's called hammering. Listen to track 15 now to get a sense of what it sounds like.

Guitarists especially like to hammer on the second of the two alternating bass strings—though whether you choose to hammer in a given place is entirely up to you. You can only hammer on a string that would normally be fingered: for example, the fourth string, second fret in an Am chord.

Here's how the move works for an Am chord. Instead of plucking the fourth string with the fretting finger in place, temporarily lift that finger (while keeping the rest of the chord shape in place) and pluck the fourth string open. Then firmly and swiftly move your fretting finger back on the second fret without muffling the note, so that the second fret note comes out without being plucked. The key to successful hammering is to make this move *decisively*, putting the fretting finger into place without muffling the string.

If you find that your other fretting fingers are muffling the open string, experiment with adjusting the angle at which your fretting fingers approach the strings. Wrist and elbow, as well as thumb position on the back of the guitar neck, may play a role here.

In the notation for this book, I use a curved line between the open note and the hammered note to indicate hammers. This line is called a *slur,* and it's the standard way of indicating this sound. In other books, you'll sometimes see the letter *h* or the abbreviation *ham* to indicate hammers.

If you're reading notes, don't confuse slurs with ties. Ties, which look the same, connect two notes *of the same pitch* to indicate that the note is held for the total duration of the tied notes. Because the connected notes are of the same pitch, you can't possibly play a hammer there. In this book, ties appear only in music notation, never in the tablature.

Track 15 is fairly long, to give you time to play along.

TRACK 15. HAMMERING ON Am

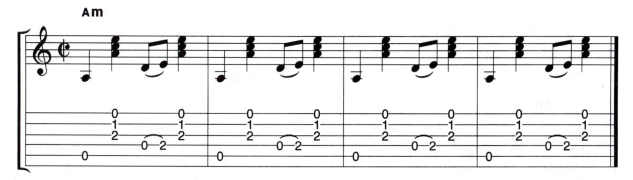

CREATIVE WORK. Practice hammering on the following chords. Use alternating-bass-style strumming, and hammer when you get to the alternate bass note, as indicated. Once you get used to hammering, practice continuously strumming a chord hammered for a while, then unhammered, then hammered, and so on.

Notice how the hammered notes give each chord a particular flavor. The B7 chord, for example, sounds bluesy, while the G and C chords have more of a country sound.

     A, Am, A7 (fourth string)

     B7 (fourth string)

     C, C7 (fourth string)

     D, Dm, D7 (third string)

     E, Em, E7 (fifth or fourth string)

     4-string F (third string)

     G, G7 (fifth string)

Track 16: Slow and Fast Hammers

The hammers I played on track 15 were even and steady. The amount of time the open-string note rang and the amount of time the hammered note lasted were equivalent. This is the way most people hammer. It's smooth, sounds good, and feels natural.

Occasionally, you'll hear a fast, twitchy-sounding hammer. The way to get this sound is to close the string more quickly. Track 16 gives an example of fast and slow hammers.

CREATIVE WORK. Practice fast and slow hammers on all the chords given in the previous example. Start thinking about which hammering style you might prefer to make your own.

LISTENING. Joan Baez generally favors a fast hammer that imparts a quality of propulsion and nervous energy. Some good examples are the songs "Lily of the West" and "Lonesome Road" from *Joan Baez, Volume 2* (Vanguard). At the other extreme, Woody Guthrie generally favored a long, lazy hammer that was as slow as his Oklahoma drawl. Listen to just about any of his work, especially *Dust Bowl Ballads* (Rounder).

Track 17: Hammering on Am and E

Track 17 provides an easy way to learn to keep your hammering steady during a chord change. Because the shapes of Am and E are identical, the hammering finger is the same in both chords. The following examples are a little harder to get used to.

TRACK 17. HAMMERING ON AM AND E

CREATIVE WORK. Keep a steady hammer going on alternating bass notes in the following chord progressions. If necessary, break out single chord changes to practice instead of working through the entire progression.

Once you get used to these progressions with hammers, experiment with leaving the hammers out on certain chords. Start thinking about when you prefer the sound of a hammered note and when you'd rather leave it unhammered, and practice the progressions accordingly.

Dm C   Am G

C   F   G7 C

G   C   G   D7

Am G   Em Am

D   A7 G   D

Track 18: Hammering in Three-Four Time

Hammering in three doesn't really differ in principle from hammering in standard time, but here's an example to get the feel of it.

Track 18. Hammering in Three-Four Time

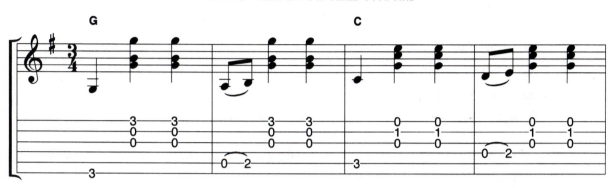

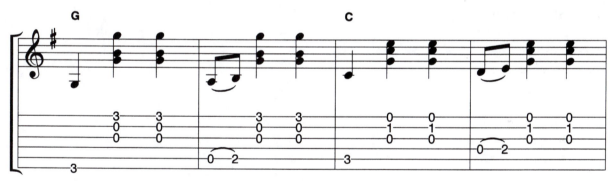

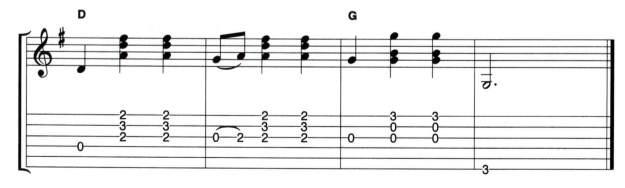

CREATIVE WORK. Practice hammering in three with the following chord changes.

G	C	G	D
G	Em	Am	D7
G	Am	C	D
D	C	G	D
Dm	F	C	D

MORE CREATIVE WORK. Notice that in the second-to-last measure of track 18, I broke my rule (maybe *policy* is a better word) about standard bass notes and went up to the open third string in the G chord. Sounds good, here, doesn't it? That's why you break the rules. Try playing the "standard" low G note (sixth string, third fret) instead. To my taste, it doesn't seem to flow as nicely out of the preceding D chord.

Go over the preceding chord-progression exercises and experiment with nonstandard bass notes. See if there are any places they sound good. *Hint:* Sometimes nonstandard bass notes sound good in a larger pattern, and you have to experiment with nonstandard notes on several chords in a row to see how they work. The possibilities are almost infinite, so it really takes a lifetime career's worth of experimenting to sort out the possibilities. But after a while, you learn how to predict what sounds good when.

EVEN MORE CREATIVE WORK. Spend the rest of your life continuing this experiment. We'll resume it in track 47.

Songs to Learn

This chapter contains eight songs. Learn them well, so you can use them as vehicles for exploring different styles.

Most teachers working with roots and other popular guitar styles take a song-based approach. Usually, the songs are simple and often include old-fashioned campfire songs and even nursery rhymes. It's good to use simple, approachable material—even "Mary Had a Little Lamb." Don't be offended by it. It's there because it's a song that almost everyone has so deeply internalized that it presents almost no learning curve as content, allowing you to focus on the guitar rather than the song itself.

Transposition

I give you each song in several keys. The technique of moving a song from one key to another is called *transposition*. Transposing makes a song sound higher or lower. It also calls for a different set of chords. Some chord shapes, as you'll see in part II, lend themselves better than others to advanced techniques of melody playing and interpretation. Therefore, the key you play a song in affects your guitar style as well as your voice.

It's not my purpose in this book to explain the theory of transposition, but I do want to give you some idea of what's going on. Here's a simple, really simplistic, explanation of the transpositions in this chapter. It won't work with chords that have sharps and flats, because sharps and flats make the arithmetic of chord relationships a little more complicated. None of the songs in this book use sharped or flatted chords.

First of all, understand that the notes in music start on the letter A, go up to G, and then start on A all over again:

A B C D E F G A B C D E F G A B C D E F G A . . . and so on

For our purposes, this means that if you want to make, say, a D note four notes higher you go to G. (Counting is always inclusive when you transpose.) Easy. And if you want to make, say, a G note four notes higher, you cycle around again past A and go to C.

So let's transpose a chord progression the chord progression C–F–G from C to D. D is one letter higher than C. Therefore, all the other letters should become one note higher to keep everything consistent.

When C becomes D, F becomes G, and G becomes A.

This is the reasoning behind transposition. You take the chord progression of a song and raise (or lower) all those chords an equivalent amount to move them into a new key.

Also remember that if the original chord is a seventh or a minor, so will the transposed chord.

Singing

Singing is the best way to learn songs, even if your interest is solely with the guitar and you have no ambition to be a singer. The words keep the song structure and feeling together in your mind while you're strumming out the chord progression. Singing helps you learn better and faster. If you're not a good singer, don't be self-conscious about it. The world is full of good guitarists who croak out songs. I'm one of them. Welcome to the club.

Singing problems can also come about when a song is too high or too low for you to sing comfortably. Different people's voices have different comfort ranges. Being a guitarist makes the problem worse because some instrumental styles require songs to be played in a certain key because the style makes use of chord shapes belonging only to that key. To a certain extent, you can lessen this problem by using a capo, but if your voice is still out of the capo's practical range, you're sunk. Sometimes this happens. Life isn't fair.

Try the following songs at first by using a simple brushing strum. Then try alternating-bass–brush accompaniments, possibly even with hammers. I perform the examples all kind of ways. You don't have to do them exactly like me.

The Songs

Track 19: Mary Had a Little Lamb

Don't be put off by this nursery song. It's important to have at least one song with melody, structure, and timing that you can assimilate without thinking about it too hard; later on you'll be using it as a vehicle for mastering some difficult techniques.

TRACK 19. MARY HAD A LITTLE LAMB

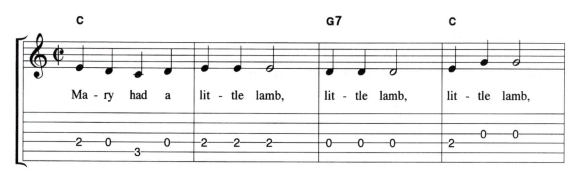

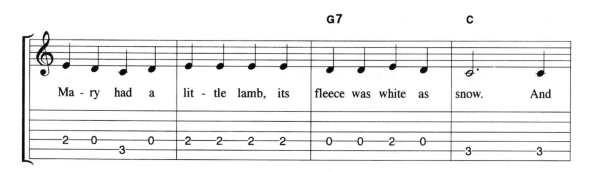

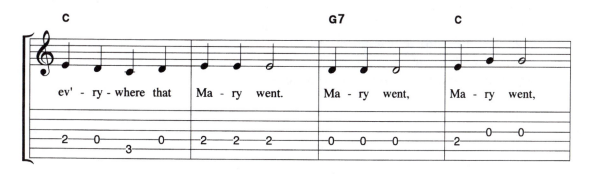

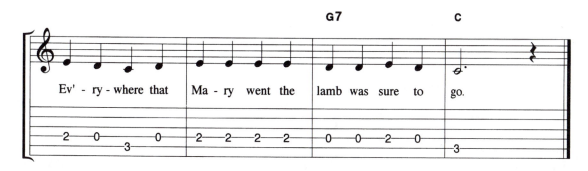

You can play this song (and the following songs) any way you like at first, but one easy approach is to just keep steady downstrokes going with your thumb or flatpick. Then, once you're familiar with the chord changes, you can try applying alternating-bass–brush strumming.

The music I've given you for "Mary Had a Little Lamb" is in the key of C. Here it is again with just the words and chords, in all the keys customarily used in American-roots guitar styles. This method of teaching a song by just showing the words and chords is handy, but it requires some engagement on your part. You need to know the melody by ear (which is why these songs appear on the CD). It also means that you need to study unfamiliar material carefully enough to accurately strum out the chords with the right number of beats.

```
C                    G7        C
Mary had a little lamb, little lamb, little lamb,
C                    G7              C
Mary had a little lamb, its fleece was white as snow.

D                    A7        D
Mary had a little lamb, little lamb, little lamb,
D                    A7              D
Mary had a little lamb, its fleece was white as snow.

E                    B7        E
Mary had a little lamb, little lamb, little lamb,
E                    B7              E
Mary had a little lamb, its fleece was white as snow.

G                    D7        G
Mary had a little lamb, little lamb, little lamb,
G                    D7              G
Mary had a little lamb, its fleece was white as snow.

A                    E7        A
Mary had a little lamb, little lamb, little lamb,
A                    E7              A
Mary had a little lamb, its fleece was white as snow.
```

CREATIVE WORK (OPTIONAL). By using some combination of the written music, your ear, and the seat of your pants, try to play the melody of "Mary Had a Little Lamb." *Hint:* Keep your left-hand fingering close to the chord shapes. Continue to try this, at your pleasure and to the best of your abilities, with the rest of the songs in this chapter. Don't worry if you don't get things perfect, and feel free to taper off or give up if you feel like it.

MORE CREATIVE WORK (OPTIONAL). Following are the words and chords to "Skip to My Lou" in the key of C. Following the model of "Mary Had a Little Lamb," transpose "Skip to My Lou" into the other four keys.

C
Lost my partner, what'll I do?
G7
Lost my partner, what'll I do?
C
Lost my partner, what'll I do?
G7   C
Skip to my Lou, my darling.

Track 20: The Cuckoo

A couple of versions of "The Cuckoo" are floating around the world of American music; the other one is slow, pretty, and in three. This version, in its native habitat, is a hard-driving, rip-roaring bit of front-porch entertainment from the southern Appalachians that's been a classic ever since Clarence "Tom" Ashley recorded it in 1929.

LISTENING. "The Coo Coo Bird" on *The Original Folkways Recordings of Doc Watson and Clarence Ashley* (Smithsonian Folkways).

TRACK 20. THE CUCKOO

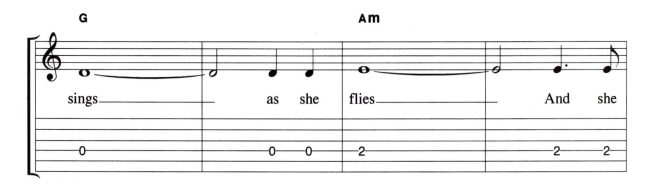

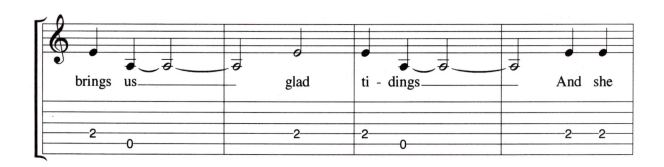

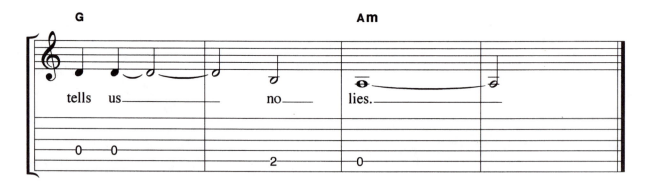

Notice in the accompaniment to the CD track how well hammering suits this song. Here it is in the key of A minor, as in the music provided. The little typographical gap between the half lines reflects the space in the phrasing of the melody. Doc Watson and Clarence Ashley, in their archetypal recordings, use the space to put in a little figure, or *fill*, on guitar or banjo.

Am	
Oh the cuckoo	she's a pretty bird
G	Am
And she sings	as she flies
Am	
And she brings us	glad tidings
G	Am
And she tells us	no lies.

She sips from	the pretty flowers
To make her	voice clear
And she never	sings cuckoo
'Til the springtime	of the year.

And here it is transposed in the key of D minor:

Dm	
Oh the cuckoo	she's a pretty bird
C	Dm
And she sings	as she flies
Dm	
And she brings us	glad tidings
D	Dm
And she tells us	no lies.

CREATIVE WORK. Learn this song in both keys with alternating-bass–brush picking, and then add hammering.

MORE CREATIVE WORK (OPTIONAL). Transpose "The Cuckoo" into the key of E minor.

Track 21: Railroad Bill

Here's another traditional song, belonging to the genre called the *badman song*. An almost-endless variety of verses to "Railroad Bill" once floated around American folk culture, each one painting a nastier portrait of the protagonist.

LISTENING. You may never have heard "Railroad Bill" before, yet there are dozens of recordings of it. Check out some of the CD-store on-line databases, and you'll see what I mean. You can even listen to streaming audio.

Two wonderful versions of this song are by Etta Baker and Taj Mahal. Hearing the two different versions by these two great stylists can teach you a lot about fingerpicking. Get the sounds in your head now so you'll be ready to approach the solo version in track 53.

Etta Baker's version is on the collection *Instrumental Music of the Southern Appalachians* (Tradition/Rykodisc). She records a slightly different version on *One Dime Blues* (Rounder). Taj Mahal's version appears on *In Progress and in Motion* (Legacy).

This song has a couple of tricky spots, both having to do with fast chord changes.

The very short G7 in the first line leaves you no space to alternate the bass note, so don't. Just play one bass-note-and-brush's worth of G7 and go back to C.

The same is true for the fast F to G change in the last line. If you're not used to going from F to G as quickly as this song requires, then go back and practice this chord change separately.

Here's a general tip for learning songs that have a tough spot in them. Don't play them too fast, causing you to suddenly put on the brakes when you come to the tough spot. That way you're only learning to play unevenly. Instead, take the whole song as slowly as you have to to get evenly over the tough spot without breaking tempo. Then bring the entire song steadily and gradually up to tempo as you master the tough spot.

TRACK 21. RAILROAD BILL

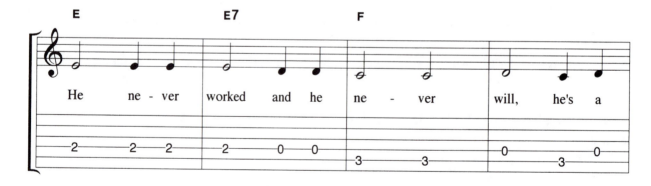

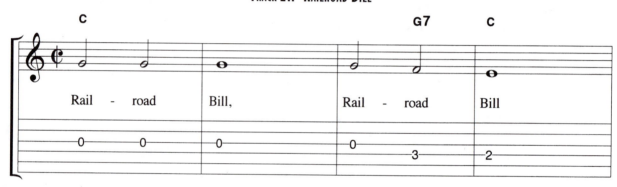

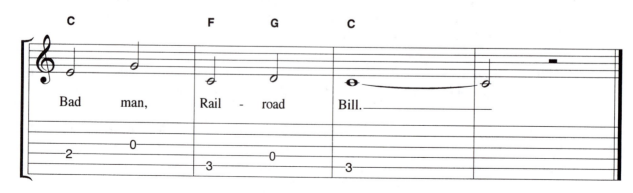

```
C                    G7   C
Railroad Bill, Railroad Bill
E        E7            F
He never worked and he never will, he's a
C      F   G    C
Bad man, Railroad Bill.
```

Railroad Bill, he's a mighty mean man
He shot the lantern out' the brakeman's hand, he's a
Bad man, Railroad Bill.

CREATIVE WORK. Learn this song with alternating bass–brush strumming.

Also try staying on the E chord instead of going to E7. Then try using an E7 instead of the E. Notice how changing a chord from its plain version to its seventh version is essentially a color change that adds spice and interest. Depending on which chord you alter, and at which place in the song, adding a seventh often adds a bluesy color. In "Railroad Bill," the E to E7 change also reflects the melody, which is why I go to the trouble of making it.

Track 22: This Little Light of Mine

"This Little Light of Mine" was originally a gospel song with chorus and verse. Now divested of its religious verses, it's often used as a rousing nonsectarian sing-along, especially with kids.

TRACK 22. THIS LITTLE LIGHT OF MINE

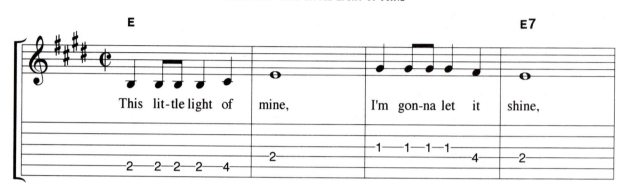

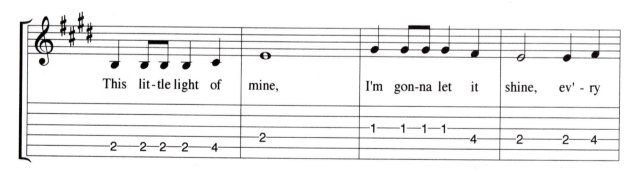

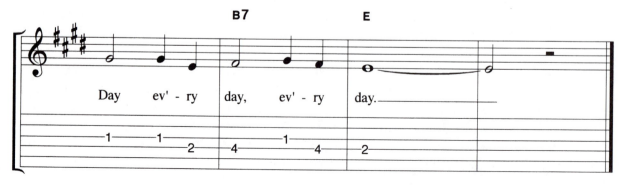

```
E                                          E7
```
This little light of mine, I'm gonna let it shine,
```
A                                          E
```
This little light of mine, I'm gonna let it shine,

This little light of mine, I'm gonna let it shine, ev'ry
```
           B7        E
```
Day, ev'ry day, ev'ry day.

Here it is in the key of G:

```
G                                          G7
```
This little light of mine, I'm gonna let it shine,
```
C                                          G
```
This little light of mine, I'm gonna let it shine,

This little light of mine, I'm gonna let it shine, ev'ry
```
           D7        G
```
Day, ev'ry day, ev'ry day.

CREATIVE WORK. Learn to play "This Little Light of Mine" with alternating-bass–brush strumming.

Notice how the E7 chord change at the end of the first line adds a bluesy color. Try leaving it out. Which version do you prefer? Try changing the E and A chords to their seventh versions at other places in the song and listen to what happens. If you like what you hear, decide where and when to make the changes. When you do this, you're *arranging* your own version of a song. Also work out your arrangement with sevenths in the key of G.

MORE CREATIVE WORK (OPTIONAL). Transpose this song into the key of A. Again, experiment with sevenths.

LISTENING. For a contemporary version in a soulful gospel-based style, listen to Sweet Honey in the Rock's *Freedom Song* on Sony. The irrepressible Raffi sings a children's version on *Rise and Shine* (Rounder). Several gospel-turned-pop singers have recorded this song, including Sam Cooke (*At the Copa*, ABKCO) and Fontella Bass (*No Ways Tired*, Nonesuch).

Track 23: Wildwood Flower

This genteel nineteenth-century parlor song entered folk tradition, where a generation or two later it found its way onto record in a version by the early country music stars The Carter Family. The Carters established this song as a persevering standard, and it became a set-piece instrumental solo. You'll learn how to play it that way later on.

The Carters' version was idiosyncratically different from the one I present here. They made the melody more bluesy, especially in the guitar part. They also strummed out an extra couple of beats after the first and second lines, but I've kept it "normal" here to make it easier to learn. Purists are no fans of this procedure—and rightfully so, from the point of view of historical accuracy—but it does make learning easier.

With exceptions, today's music generally regiments itself in even, regular units of beats. Early blues and old-time country musicians often arranged their songs with "extra" beats in between, or sometimes within, the sung lines. Even some dance tunes sometimes incorporated an extra beat or two as part of the dance step—they called it a *backstep*. But right now, let's devote our energies to learning songs that serve our progress on the guitar and not on unusual ways of playing them.

LISTENING. There must be a hundred versions of this song on CD in various folk, country, and bluegrass styles. The archetypal, idiosyncratic Carter Family version has been reissued on several CDs, including *Can the Circle Be Unbroken* (Legacy).

Bluegrass guitarist Tony Rice plays a graceful version with mandolinist David Grisman on their *Tone Poems* album (Acoustic Disc).

Woody Guthrie wrote new words, and changed around the melody, in his World War II–era song "The Sinking of the Reuben James" on several albums, including *The Asch Recordings, Vol. 1* (Smithsonian Folkways).

Track 23. Wildwood Flower

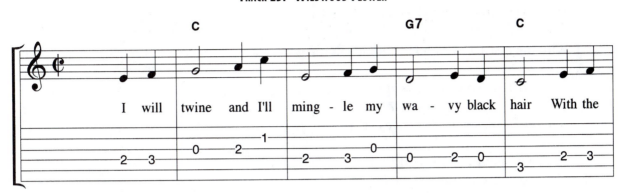

I will twine and I'll ming - le my wa - vy black hair With the

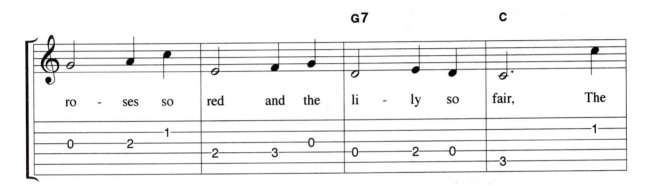

ro - ses so red and the li - ly so fair, The

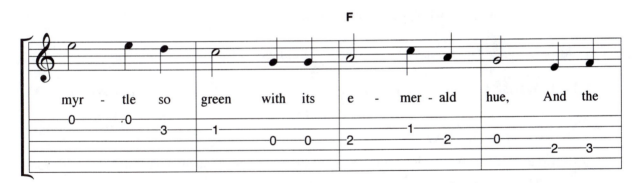

myr - tle so green with its e - mer - ald hue, And the

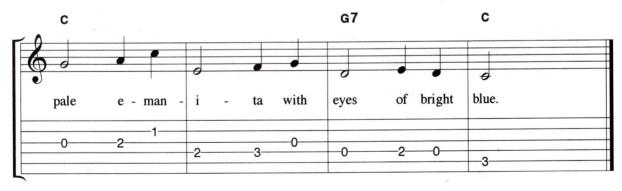

pale e - man - i - ta with eyes of bright blue.

```
     C                        G7        C
I will twine and I'll mingle my wavy black hair
        C                   G7   C
With the roses so red and the lily so fair,
                          F      C
The myrtle so green with its emerald hue,
                         G7        C
And the pale emanita with eyes of bright blue.
```

I will dance and I'll sing and my heart will be gay,
I'll banish this weeping, drive troubles away,
I'll live yet to see him regret this dark hour
When he won and neglected this frail wildwood flower.

Here's "Wildwood Flower" in G:

```
     G                      D7       G
I will twine and I'll mingle my wavy black hair
        G                 D7   G
With the roses so red and the lily so fair,
                          C      G
The myrtle so green with its emerald hue,
                         D7        C
And the pale emanita with eyes of bright blue.
```

CREATIVE WORK. Learn this song with alternating-bass–brush accompaniment.

MORE CREATIVE WORK (OPTIONAL). Transpose this song into at least one of these keys: E, A, D.

Track 24. Crawdad Song

Crawdads are crayfish, a delicious southern delicacy and once also a valued source of food and income in an impoverished economy.

LISTENING. This song has been recorded by such varied (and unlikely) artists as country singer/actor Andy Griffith, original rockabilly artist Jerry Lee Lewis, and swing-era blues shouter Joe Turner. Check out Doc Watson's version on *The Original Folkways Recordings of Doc Watson and Clarence Ashley* (Smithsonian Folkways).

Track 24. Crawdad Song

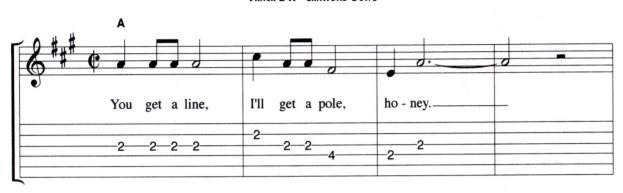

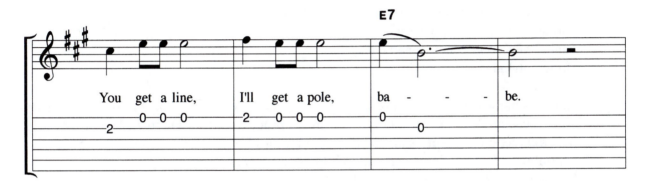

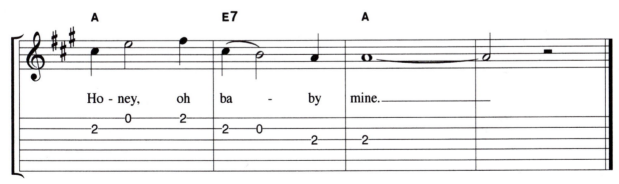

A
You get a line, I'll get a pole, honey.
                                              E7
You get a line, I'll get a pole, babe.
A
You get a line, I'll get a pole,
D7
We'll go down to the crawdad hole,
A   E7   A
Honey, oh baby mine.

Yonder come a man with a sack on his back, honey.
Yonder come a man with a sack on his back, babe.
Yonder come a man with a sack on his back
Packin' all the crawdads he can pack,
Honey, oh baby mine.

Here it is in the key of C. To make life easier for you, I've changed what "should" be F7 into a plain F, causing it to lose its bluesy flavor in the process. Folk guitarists make compromises in the direction of easiness all the time. Sometimes laziness actually leads to interesting-sounding and original discoveries. Sometimes, like now, it doesn't.

C
You get a line, I'll get a pole, honey.
                                              G7
You get a line, I'll get a pole, babe.
C
You get a line, I'll get a pole,
F
We'll go down to the crawdad hole,
C   G7   C
Honey, oh baby mine.

CREATIVE WORK. Learn this song in alternating-bass–brush style. Then try it with hammers. Make sure you learn it in C as well as A—you'll be doing advanced versions in both keys later on.

In the key of A, notice how bluesy the D7 sounds. Try a plain D instead. Which do you prefer? If you like the bluesy sound, try making A chords into A7 chords some of the time. *Hint:* It doesn't have to be for the entire duration of the A chord. Part of the A chord time could be A7; part of it could still be A.

MORE CREATIVE WORK (OPTIONAL). Transpose this song into G and E.

Track 25: On Top of Old Smoky

By the 1960s, this love lament in three-quarter time from (presumably) the Great Smoky Mountains had turned into a campfire-song staple of the folk-song revival. It was so over-sung that it became hackneyed, and people stopped singing it. Maybe it's time to take another look at its beautiful melody and poignant lyrics. Besides, it's going to turn into a useful song for our learning purposes.

LISTENING. The Weavers sing a classic campfire-song version on *Best of the Weavers* (Vanguard). Country comedienne Minnie Pearl does an energetic take-off on the collection *All Time Country and Western Hits* (King). Folk revivalist Spider John Koerner offers a bluesy honky-tonk version on *Raised by Humans* (Red House).

TRACK 25. ON TOP OF OLD SMOKY

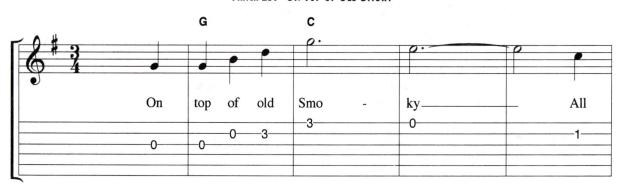

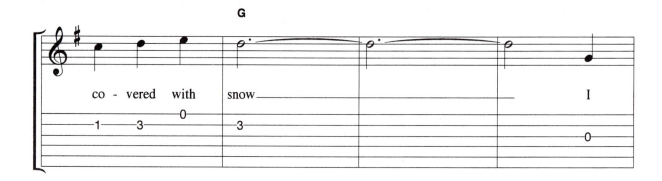

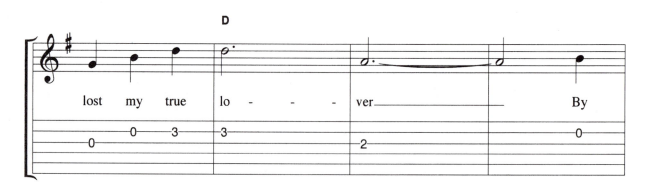

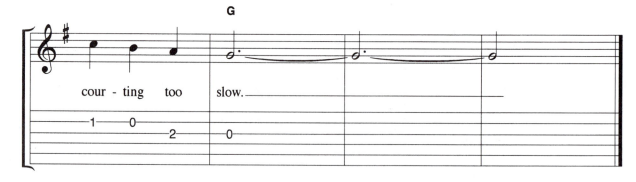

```
    G         C
On top of Old Smoky
                 G
All covered with snow
             D
I lost my true lover
                 G
By courting too slow.
```

Now courting's a pleasure
And parting's a grief
But a false hearted lover
Is worse than a thief.

For a thief he will rob you
And take what you have
But a false hearted lover
Will lead you to the grave.

The grave will decay you
And turn you to dust
Not one man in a thousand
That a poor girl can trust.

You'll also be playing this song later in C:

```
    C         F
On top of Old Smoky
                 C
All covered with snow
             G
I lost my true lover
                 C
By courting too slow.
```

CREATIVE WORK. Learn this song with the alternating-bass–brush–brush accompaniment and try hammering on the chords. Decide whether you prefer to hammer at every opportunity, or just some, or none at all.

MORE CREATIVE WORK (OPTIONAL). Transpose this song into A and D.

Track 26: Cripple Creek

Fiddle tunes generally have a characteristic form. A fiddle tune is usually instrumental but sometimes come equipped, like this one, with trivial, fun words for singing. Because this one has words, I'll describe the form in terms of its sung lines for convenience. First comes a melody (lines 1–2), which is repeated (lines 3–4). Then comes a second melody (lines 5–6), which is also repeated (lines 7–8). The resulting melodic form is AABB.

There are exceptions, of course, but most fiddle tunes in European and American cultures, some going as far back as the Middle Ages, share this form.

LISTENING. "Cripple Creek" is a standard that's been recorded in many styles but not, to the best of my knowledge, the styles we play it in in this book. No matter.

Contemporary fingerpicking guitar stylist Leo Kottke has recorded it on *Standing in My Shoes* (Private Music) and several other CDs. A classic bluegrass version is the elegant one by Lester Flatt and Earl Scruggs on their *20 All-Time Greatest Recordings* (Columbia). Hobart Smith, a wonderful old-time fiddler, does a version like no one else's on the collection *Instrumental Music of the Southern Appalachians* (Tradition/Rykodisc).

Track 26. Cripple Creek

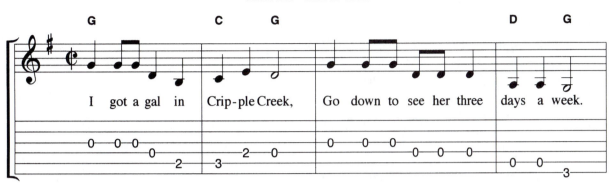

I got a gal in Crip-ple Creek, Go down to see her three days a week.

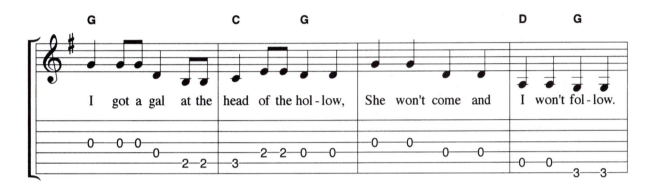

I got a gal at the head of the hol-low, She won't come and I won't fol-low.

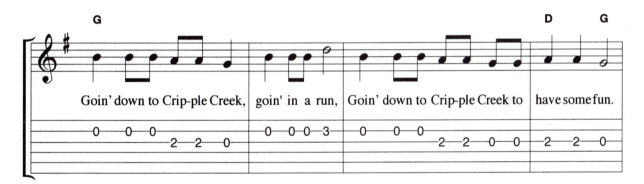

Goin' down to Crip-ple Creek, goin' in a run, Goin' down to Crip-ple Creek to have some fun.

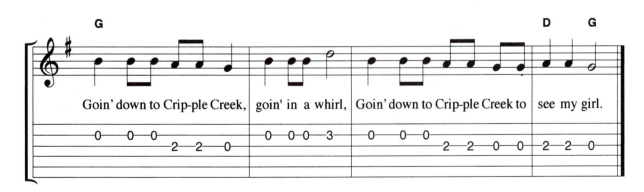

Goin' down to Crip-ple Creek, goin' in a whirl, Goin' down to Crip-ple Creek to see my girl.

```
G          C        G
I got a gal in Cripple Creek,
                            D        G
Go down to see her three days a week.
G          C        G
I got a gal at the head of the hollow,
                          D        G
She won't come and I won't follow.


G
Goin' down to Cripple Creek, goin' in a run,
                              D          G
Goin' down to Cripple Creek to have some fun.
G
Goin' down to Cripple Creek, goin' in a whirl,
                              D       G
Goin' down to Cripple Creek to see my girl.
```

Later on, you'll also be working with "Cripple Creek" in the key of A:

```
A          D        A
I got a gal in Cripple Creek,
                          E        A
Go down to see her three days a week.
A          D        A
I got a gal at the head of the hollow,
                        E        A
She won't come and I won't follow.


A
Goin' down to Cripple Creek, goin' in a run,
                              E          A
Goin' down to Cripple Creek to have some fun.
A
Goin' down to Cripple Creek, goin' in a whirl,
                              E          A
Goin' down to Cripple Creek to see my girl.
```

CREATIVE WORK. Learn this song with the alternating-bass–brush strum. Notice how you just don't have time to play alternating bass notes on any but the G chord (or A, in the transposition).

MORE CREATIVE WORK (OPTIONAL). Transpose this song into the keys of C and E. You'll notice that the key of E calls for a B chord, but you may not know B (and if you do, you know it's a pain to play). Use B7 instead.

7

More Flat-picking
and Fingerpicking Patterns

The Bump-Diddy Pattern

Track 27: Bump-Diddy in C

Let's develop the bass-brush strumming pattern a little more fully.

Drummers use silly words like *flam* and *paradiddle* to describe the sounds they make and so, sometimes, do guitarists. *Bump-diddy* is a good word to describe the *one-and-a, two-and-a* feeling of the beat you hear in track 27. You may feel silly saying *bump-diddy,* and so do I, but it works. (We live in undignified times, in any case.)

Listen to track 27, and you'll hear that the three components of bump-diddy aren't equally long. If you listen to yourself carefully when you say "bump-diddy" you'll notice that the "bump" uses up half the entire time it takes you to say it, while the "did" and the "dy" each take up a quarter of the time.

To produce the bump-diddy beat, just add a quick upstroke after the downward brush stroke in the bass-brush pattern.

If you're using a flat pick, your picking pattern is *down + down + up.*

If you're using bare fingers or bare fingers plus thumb pick, your picking pattern is *thumb + index down + index up.* Back when you were first working on the bass-brush pattern, I suggested that, if you wished, you could make your downward brush stroke either with the index finger alone or with two or three fingers. You'll probably find, however, that you prefer to do the bump-diddy beat with just your index finger.

If you like to use thumb pick plus finger picks, you'll find that the most fluent way to express the bump-diddy rhythm is completely different than with bare fingers. Play the bass

55

note with a thumb stroke. Then play the first brush (the "did") with another downward stroke of the thumb, and the second brush (the "dy") with upward stroke of the index finger.

TRACK 27. BUMP-DIDDY IN C

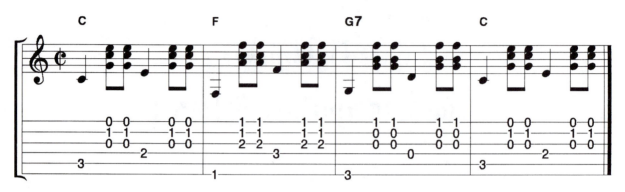

CREATIVE WORK. Go back to chord-progression exercises from previous chapters and play them with the bump-diddy rhythm until you feel comfortable. Then go over all the songs except "On Top of Old Smoky" and learn them with the bump-diddy rhythm.

Just because bump-diddy is more complicated than the simple bass-brush stroke, it's not necessarily better. Start thinking about whether any songs sound more pleasing to you using just the bass-brush pattern.

Track 28: Bump-Diddy-Diddy in D

Playing the bump-diddy rhythm in three is easy. Just add another diddy. (Of course, you'll feel a third again sillier saying "bump-diddy-diddy" than you do saying "bump-diddy," but let's not worry about that.)

TRACK 28. BUMP-DIDDY-DIDDY IN D

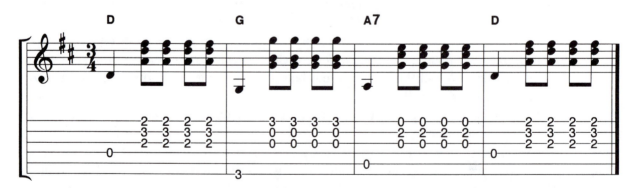

CREATIVE WORK. In this track, each chord is held for only three beats, so you don't have the opportunity to play alternating bass notes. Rework this selection, repeating each chord for a total duration of six beats per chord, so you have time to play the alternating bass notes.

MORE CREATIVE WORK. Go back over as many previous chord-progression exercises as you need in order to get this pattern fluent. Then apply it to "On Top of Old Smoky" (track 25).

Track 29: Hammering with Bump-Diddy on Am and G

When you incorporate a hammer into the bump-diddy strum, it creates an even, flowing rhythm of four equal components that sounds like *bump-a-diddy.* But because only the alternating bass note gets the hammer, the total effect of a whole strumming cycle is more like *bump-diddy, bump-a-diddy.*

TRACK 29. HAMMERING WITH BUMP-DIDDY ON AM AND G

CREATIVE WORK. Play this rhythm first with individual chords, then with chord progressions from previous chapters, until you're fluent with it. Then apply this rhythm to all the songs from chapter 6.

MORE CREATIVE WORK. Remember that adding the hammer makes the rhythm fancier but not necessarily better. Some songs may sound better with hammering, some without. Making these decisions is part of the art of arranging a song. It's a lifelong process. There's no reason you can't start making these decisions now.

LISTENING. Go back again to the three guitarists I first suggested in track 5: Jimmie Rodgers, Woody Guthrie, and Doc Watson. Listen for each guitarist's individual style and notice when they play just downstrokes and when they use upstrokes (e.g., Jimmie Rodgers is *all* downstrokes, even when he sounds like he's using upstroke rhythms, and Doc Watson uses upstrokes in more places than we're using here.)

For a taste of history, add more great guitarists, both seminal and recent: Mother Maybelle Carter with the Carter Family; Bob Dylan, especially his early recordings, the first (unaccompanied) set on *Live 1966* (Legacy), and any other songs where he isn't too covered up by a band, so you can hear what an artful strummer he is; and Tony Rice, the contemporary bluegrass stylist who can be heard clearly on the *Tone Poems* album with David Grisman (*Acoustic Disc*).

Pattern Picking

Now you're going to enter the world of *fingerpicking,* or *fingerstyle guitar.* People use these words different ways, so there's no point in looking for consistency. What's consistent about the style you're going to be using is that it's based on orderly patterns of movement in the picking hand.

Fingerpicking, as I and others use the term, refers to a style of playing in which the thumb constantly alternates between two bass strings while the fingers play notes on the high strings. You'll be applying this style to melody playing starting with track 48. In the meantime, learn a simple accompaniment pattern. It should sound familiar. You've heard Bob Dylan, Joan Baez, Paul Simon, and hundreds of other guitarists all play their versions of this pattern—or even the exact pattern we're about to learn.

Track 30: Preparatory Exercise for Pattern Picking

This is a preparatory exercise. It's pleasing but repetitive. Learn it and then move on. Notice how the pattern works. The thumb alternates between the two bass strings. In between the thumb notes, the first and second fingers alternately pluck the second and first strings.

Before you start playing, position your picking hand. Finger a C chord. Put your thumb on the fifth string. Put your first finger on the second string and your second finger on your first string. That's the position your picking hand needs to be in for this style.

TRACK 30. PREPARATORY EXERCISE FOR PATTERN PICKING

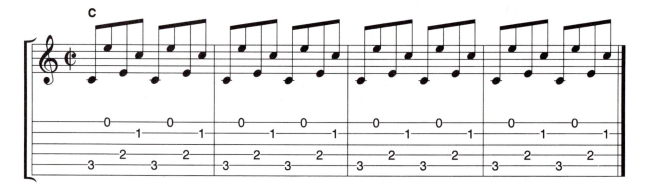

CREATIVE WORK. Play this pattern at first on every chord you know, always taking care that your thumb plays the appropriate bass notes for each chord. On the D, Dm, and D7 chords, most guitarists use the alternating bass strings 5,4. (Few players choose to reverse the usual low-high thumb alternation in order to play the "preferable" 4,5 alternation.)

Pick this pattern on the following progressions:

C Am C Am (bass strings 5,4 throughout)

G Em G Em (bass strings 6,4 throughout)

A D   A D (bass strings 5,4 throughout)

F Dm F Dm (4-string F using bass strings 4,3 throughout)

Track 31: Pattern Picking

Less is often more in guitar playing, and that's certainly true here. Our preparatory exercise used one finger stroke in between every thumb stroke—four finger strokes for every four thumb strokes.

Now you're just going to cut out two of those four finger strokes. It's easier to play than to describe in detail.

TRACK 31. PATTERN PICKING

CREATIVE WORK. Practice this rhythm on various chords of your choice. Try it on these chord progressions, which you used earlier with track 30:

C Am C Am (bass strings 5,4 throughout)

G Em G Em (bass strings 6,4 throughout)

A D   A D (bass strings 5,4 throughout)

F Dm F Dm (4-string F and bass strings 4,3 throughout)

Track 32: Picking on a Chord Progression

Some people have no trouble pattern picking across a chord progression where the alternating bass notes change from chord to chord, but others find it tricky. Play as slowly as you have to to master the chord changes evenly.

TRACK 32. PICKING ON A CHORD PROGRESSION

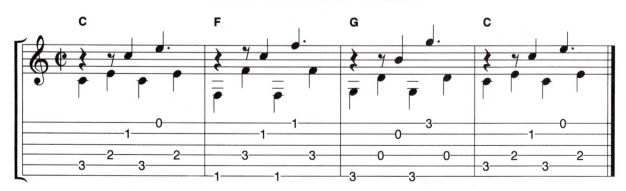

CREATIVE WORK. Practice this pattern on various chord changes and chord progressions of your choice.

MORE CREATIVE WORK. Once you get the pattern into your fingers, apply it to all the songs from chapter 6 except "On Top of Old Smoky." (There's no picking pattern in general use for three-four time.) You may feel that some songs work very well with pattern picking, while others sound more pleasing to you with a bass-brush approach. You'll have to decide whether to take a strumming or fingerpicking approach every time you learn a new song.

A word of caution: Every so often you'll find a song where a chord change comes so fast that you have to make it right in the middle of the picking cycle. This happens twice in "Railroad Bill." (Review the commentary on that song in track 21, which discusses the fast chord changes.) Practice the fast C-to-G7 and F-to-G chord changes separately until you master them before trying to pick the song all the way through. And don't play at so fast a tempo that it becomes uneven when you get to those chord changes.

Look elsewhere for some songs to try this pattern with—especially classics that for copyright reasons can't be included here. You'll find that pattern picking suits songs like Simon and Garfunkel's "The Boxer," Dylan's "Don't Think Twice, It's All Right." Jackson Browne's "Take It Easy" (best known in a version by the Eagles), and Steve Goodman's "City of New Orleans" (best known in a version by Arlo Guthrie).

Track 33: Pattern Picking with a Pinch

Careers have been built on pattern picking simply as we know it already, but I want to add one more variation. Don't proceed with this track until you're comfortable with pattern picking as developed in the last track.

Pinching is an aptly descriptive term for the gesture you make when you produce two notes simultaneously by plucking down with your thumb and up with a finger. Try it with your thumb and index finger on the fifth and second strings of a C chord. Sure enough, it's a pinch.

Pinching adds an extra high note to the picking pattern. This can make for some interesting variation.

TRACK 33. PATTERN PICKING WITH A PINCH

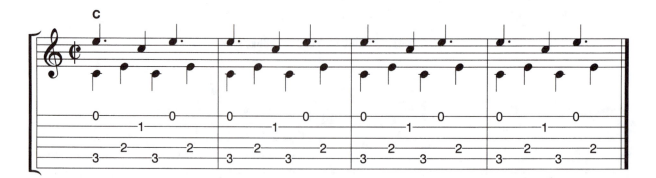

CREATIVE WORK. Try pinching on various chords of your choice. Now try going back and forth between pattern picking with and without a pinch. At first, just go back and forth randomly between pinching and not pinching. Then, as you gain control, work toward strictly alternating pinched and nonpinched versions of the pattern, just to show your fingers who's boss.

Track 34: Pinching on a Chord Progression

Now try the pinch on a chord progression. This can be trickier than you might think because to get in that first pinched note, you really have to be on top of swift, clean chord changes. Any weaknesses you have in making chord changes are going to show up now, so single them out and give them extra attention as they appear.

TRACK 34. PINCHING ON A CHORD PROGRESSION

CREATIVE WORK. Use pinched and unpinched pattern-picking accompaniment on all the songs from chapter 6, including original and transposed keys, except for "On Top of Old Smoky." Which songs sound better to you pinched, and which do not? Also continue thinking about which songs sound better to you with fingerpicked accompaniment, and which sound better to you strummed instead.

MORE CREATIVE WORK. Try the pinched pattern picking on the following chord progression, and then try it without pinches:

 C Em Am C

Notice that all these chords have the same high note on the open first string. Using pinches makes that note repeat so much that it becomes boring. The unpinched version actually sounds more interesting—to my ear, at least.

Now try this chord progression both pinched and unpinched:

 C G F C

Here, the high notes change from chord to chord. They form an interesting pattern.

You now have a lifetime of decision making ahead of you. Go over past chord progressions and songs and start thinking about whether you want to pinch or not pinch. Remember, there are no rights and wrongs here. You're simply starting down the road to your personal style.

There's also an easy way out. Many guitarists are perfectly happy to go through their entire lives using only the unpinched version of pattern picking. If you feel overwhelmed by the decisions posed in this track, then this is the course you should take—at least for the time being.

LISTENING. You'll hear plenty of pattern picking in the work of singer-songwriters, and especially in the early work of Bob Dylan, Paul Simon, Joan Baez, and others in the time when it was still fashionable to record with only a solo guitar accompaniment. You're also ready to start studying the work of real virtuoso players like Doc Watson, John Hurt, Etta Baker, Merle Travis, and Chet Atkins—again, their early work where the solo guitar is really exposed. You'll notice, even in their complex styles, the persistence and repetition of certain picking patterns, including the very ones in this chapter.

PART

II

Guitar Styles

Old-Time, Bluegrass, and Early Country Styles

In this chapter, you'll learn two important developments of the bass-brush accompaniment style. You can play them either pick or finger style. First, you'll play bass runs—little connecting melodic figures that link one chord to another. Then you're going to play melodies. Both the bass runs and melodies will be accompanied brush strokes.

Bass Runs

Track 35: Bass Runs in C

Begin by listening to this track a few times. Notice the way the notes of the bass run connect one chord to another. Get a feel for the timing: *bass-brush-bass-bass*.

The track includes two separate sets of bass runs. The first set comes over chord changes that move quickly, the other over the same chord changes with the chords held longer to give you time to play alternating bass notes. There's no difference in the actual bass runs themselves.

TRACK 35. BASS RUNS IN C

Part 1: Quick Chord Changes

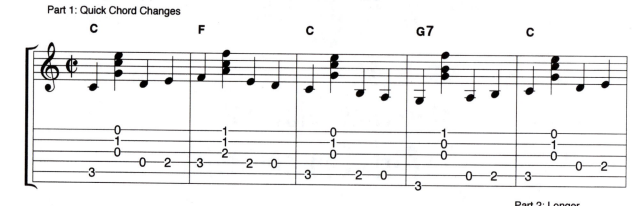

Part 2: Longer
Chord Changes

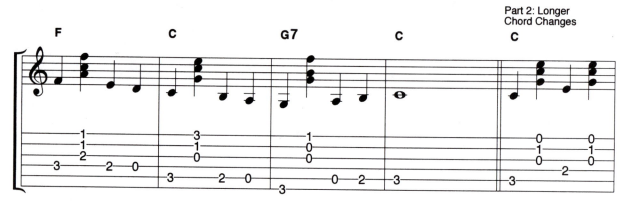

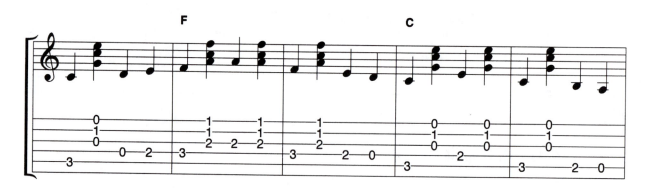

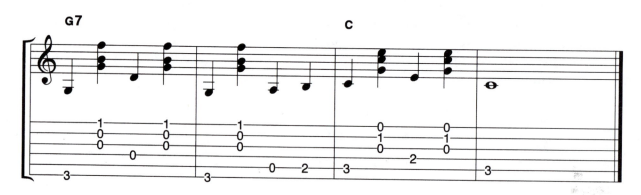

Now that you've played the runs a few times, notice the similarity in the fingering shapes of the runs. The moves from C to F and back are identical (on strings 5,4) to the moves from G7 to C and back (on strings 6,5). Continue to play these bass runs until you're familiar with them.

CREATIVE WORK. Play the bass runs with G instead of G7. The runs are identical.

Track 36: Crawdad Song, Accompanied by Bass Runs

Review "Crawdad Song" on track 24.

Bass runs aren't too hard to learn, but learning just where to place them in a given song comes only from experience. Each song is its own special case. You need to think ahead so you can time the run to end on the first note of the new chord change. Sometimes it takes a little experimenting, and some songs are harder than others to feel out.

Bass runs also create a singing problem for some people because they can pull your voice off course. Work on getting comfortable with the sung melody and the bass runs separately before you combine them.

Track 36 provides an accompaniment to the "Crawdad Song." Notice how it works; you just keep on playing standard alternating bass notes until it's time to start the run. The last G7 chord is too short to have alternating bass notes.

TRACK 36.　CRAWDAD SONG, ACCOMPANIED BY BASS RUNS

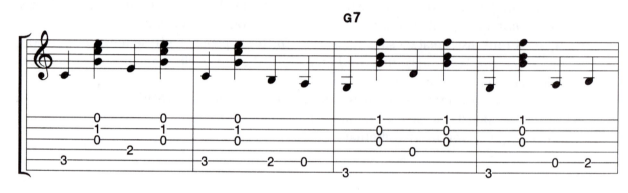

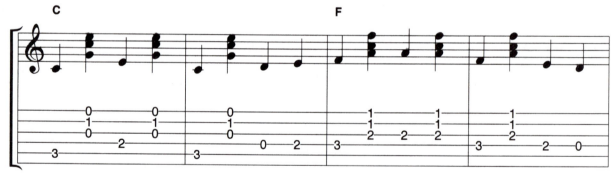

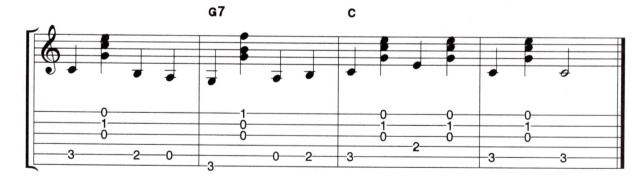

CREATIVE WORK. Figure out bass runs in the key of C for "Mary Had a Little Lamb."

Track 37: Bass Runs in A

You're not going to learn bass runs in every key here, but let's go over those for A. They're easy to grasp because, like C, bass runs in the key of A are similar in shape. Going back and forth from A to D uses the same fingering shapes on strings 5,4 as those going from E to A on strings 6,5.

The A bass runs are a little harder to play because you need to break away from the chord shapes in order to play them. Use whatever fingers feel natural to you. *Hint:* Once you decide on the fingering you like, keep on using that fingering consistently.

TRACK 37. BASS RUNS IN A

Part 1: Quick Chord Changes

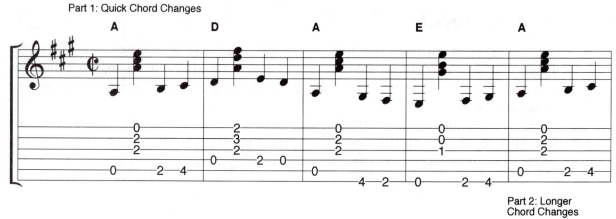

Part 2: Longer
Chord Changes

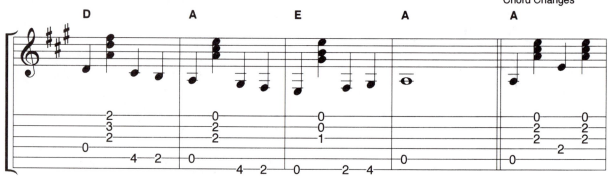

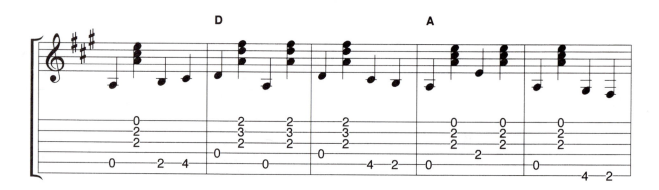

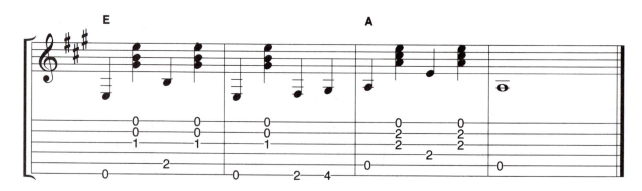

CREATIVE WORK. Play this exercise with E7 instead of E. The run is the same.

MORE CREATIVE WORK. Play "Mary Had a Little Lamb" and "Crawdad Song" in the key of A, using these runs.

Track 38: Cripple Creek, Accompanied by Bass Runs

Review track 26. Then work on this track.

   Notice how the chord changes in "Cripple Creek" move so fast that there's just no time to put in bass runs leading out of the chords. I'm only using bass runs leading into chords. When songs don't have enough space to put in bass runs, don't put them in. It's simple.

TRACK 38. CRIPPLE CREEK, ACCOMPANIED BY BASS RUNS

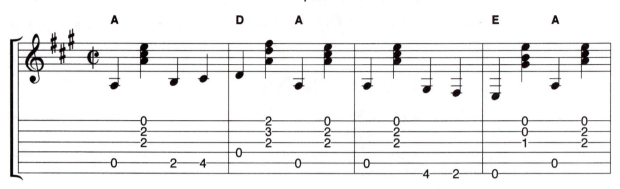

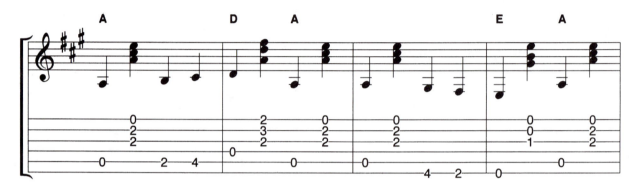

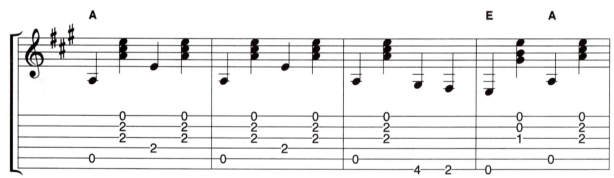

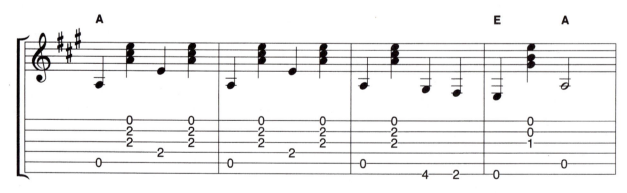

CREATIVE WORK. Play "Cripple Creek" in the key of C with bass runs. Then play "Crawdad Song" in the key of A with bass runs.

Over time, experiment with bass runs in all the songs from chapter 6 in the keys of C and A. You can also try the key of G. You haven't learned bass runs to and from D or D7, but you do know how to get from G to C and back.

Be patient. There are pitfalls. Bass runs may be hard to work into some songs. *Hint:* Feel free to decide that a song just doesn't seem to work with bass runs, and don't try. You're probably right.

Try to learn bass runs with as many songs as possible, and use them in every possible place. Then back off. It's possible to overuse bass runs. Guitarists often arrange songs with about half as many bass runs as they could possibly fit in. Or they just skip them entirely.

Go back to "Crawdad Song," track 36. Instead of using a bass run from the final G7 back to C, put in an alternating bass note and brush instead. How do you like this?

MORE CREATIVE WORK. Go back over all the songs you've been playing with bass runs, and this time incorporate hammers into the alternating bass notes. Then do them with the bump-diddy beat.

Track 39: Bass Runs in Three-Four Time

Bass runs feel very different in three. They take up three whole beats.

TRACK 39. BASS RUNS IN THREE-FOUR TIME

CREATIVE WORK. Play this exercise staying on each chord twice as long, so you have time to play alternating bass notes. Then figure out how to play this exercise in the key of A. Then double the chord duration in A as well.

Track 40: On Top of Old Smoky, Accompanied by Bass Runs

"On Top of Old Smoky" sounds very natural accompanied by bass runs, but it's a little tricky to sing over them. Give it a try.

Track 40. On Top of Old Smoky, Accompanied by Bass Runs

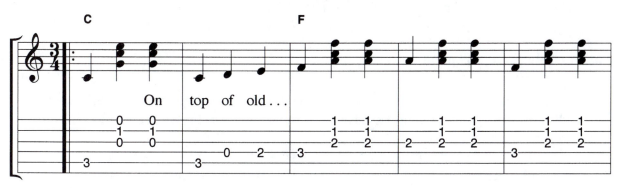

On   top of old . . .

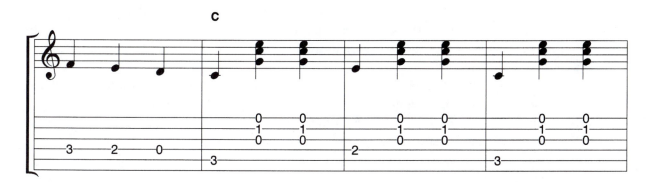

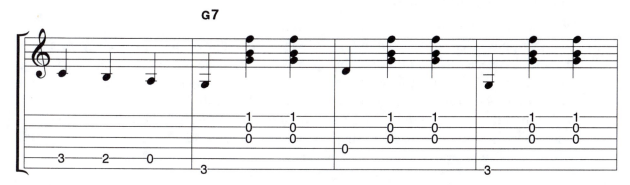

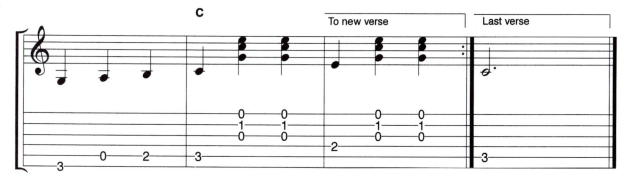

CREATIVE WORK. Play "On Top of Old Smoky" in A with bass runs. Also try it in G, remembering that you only know the runs to and from C but not to and from D.

Carter-Style Melody Playing

Carter-style playing is named after Maybelle Carter. As a member of the legendary Carter Family, she was one of country music's first radio and recording stars and one of its most influential guitar stylists.

The principle is simple. Instead of playing alternating bass notes, you pluck out the melody notes of the song. Whenever you need to, you omit the brush and play a melody note instead.

The art of playing in this style consists of making good choices. If you leave out too many brush strokes, you lose your rhythmic thrust and the sound of the chord. But if brushing makes you leave out too many melody notes, you lose the flow of the melody. It's all about compromise.

Some songs lend themselves better than others to this approach, so another part of the art is picking your songs carefully. It also helps to understand which keys and chord shapes best express a given song. That comes from experience. *Hint:* C and G are generally the keys that work most easily in this style.

Track 41: Cripple Creek, Carter Style

Review the sung version of "Cripple Creek" on track 26.

"Cripple Creek" works well in Carter style. It's possible to play this piece with a good balance between melody notes and brushes. Notice how the melody is just a skeleton; instead of reflecting every syllable of the words, it has just enough bare bones to suggest the shape of the sung tune. Then it gets fleshed out with brush strokes.

When the melody requires you to move or remove a finger from a chord shape, keep the fingers for the rest of the chord shape in place as much as possible. Don't lose track of the chord shape, whatever you do—you'll need to have it in place for the strums.

TRACK 41. CRIPPLE CREEK, CARTER STYLE

CREATIVE WORK. For the fourth note into the song, try substituting a brush stroke. Try the same on the second note in the first C chord. How do you like these choices? Do you mind losing the melodic thread? Or are you willing to give up the melody notes in return for the chord sound and rhythm of the brushes?

Play this arrangement with a D7 instead of D. Which do you prefer?

MORE CREATIVE WORK (OPTIONAL). This is demanding. Transpose the song into the key of C and then try to figure out how to play a Carter-style arrangement in that key. Don't be afraid to fumble around until you get it; it's the only way to learn. *Hint:* Your starting note is within the C chord, second string, first fret. Review bass runs in C. They'll help you find fingerings.

Track 42: Wildwood Flower, Carter Style

Review the sung version of "Wildwood Flower" on track 23, including the commentary.

"Wildwood Flower" is a classic piece that epitomizes the Carter style. Although its nineteenth-century lyric is now unfashionable, it's been recorded as an instrumental countless times, and for decades it has been a set piece by which budding country guitarists measure their prowess.

This is a harder piece to play than "Cripple Creek" because you have to move your fingers around more. At the same time, it's repetitious and has a symmetrical melody, so it's easier to assimilate once you get the fingerings down.

As usual, work off chord shapes. To play the second note of the song, for example, keep the C chord in place and drop your pinky onto the fourth string, third fret. To play the fifth note of the song, the one right after the first chord brush, keep the C chord in shape except for your middle finger, which you'll have to take off the fourth string and move to cover the third string, second fret.

TRACK 42. WILDWOOD FLOWER, CARTER STYLE

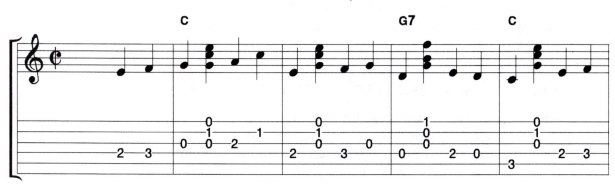

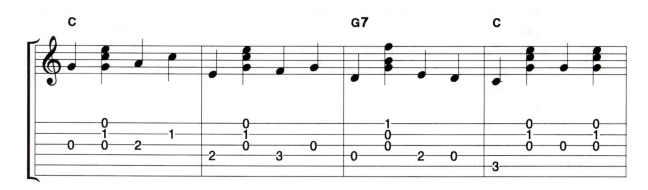

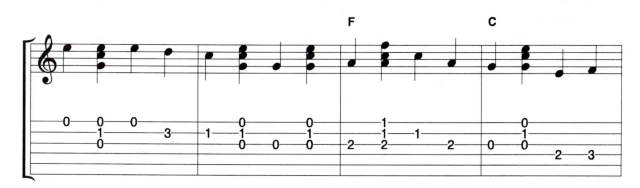

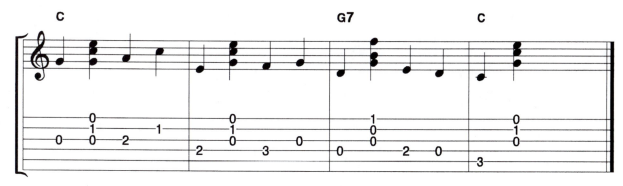

CREATIVE WORK. Play G instead of G7. Which do you prefer?

Learn this piece again using the bump-diddy pattern instead of the simple bass-brush. Then apply the bump-diddy pattern to the preceding track, "Cripple Creek." Do you have a preference?

Track 43: Wildwood Flower, Carter Style with Hammered Notes

Review the technique of hammering, tracks 15–18.

You originally learned to hammer on chord shapes, going from an open to a closed string. In track 43, you're also going to start the hammer on a closed string using the pinky, as in the third written measure. Take it easy; it's possible to strain a weak pinky with too much practice.

You may find the third-string hammers on the F chord hard to execute cleanly because the ring finger playing the fourth string gets in the way. There's an easy solution. Don't bother fingering the fourth string. You don't need it in this arrangement.

Hammering really sounds great with Carter-style playing, but if you find this arrangement overly challenging to play, feel free to put it on the back burner and move ahead to the next track.

TRACK 43. WILDWOOD FLOWER, CARTER STYLE WITH HAMMERED NOTES

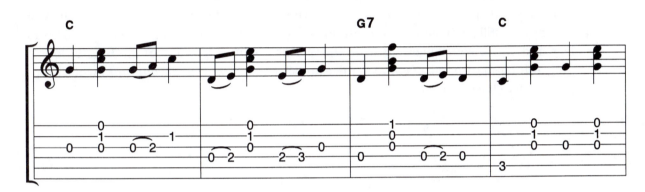

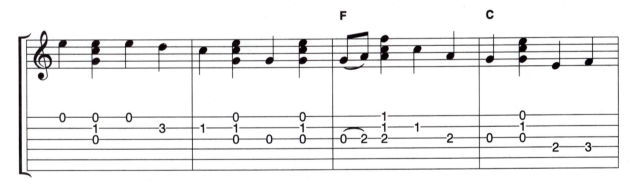

CREATIVE WORK. Rework this arrangement including both hammering and the bump-diddy beat. Go back to "Cripple Creek" (track 38) and find the one good place to hammer. Give it a try.

This arrangement for "Wildwood Flower" has hammers in just about every possible place. Try leaving some out. How do you like it that way?

Track 44: Skip to My Lou, Carter Style

Here, I've written out the literal melody of "Skip to My Lou," followed by a simple Carter-style version so that you can see with this very easy song what goes on in the creative process of making over a song into this style. Again, there's only a skeleton melody in order to make room for some strumming.

In creating a Carter-style arrangement, you first learn the chords and the basic melody. Typically, you'd figure out the melody by ear. Then you decide how much of the melody you can play and still get in enough strumming to suit you. As always, keep the chord shapes in place and derive your fingerings from them. This applies especially to the F note (fourth string, third fret) with the G7 chord in measure 12. *Play this note with your pinky* while keeping the rest of the G7 in place.

TRACK 44. SKIP TO MY LOU, CARTER STYLE

Literal melody

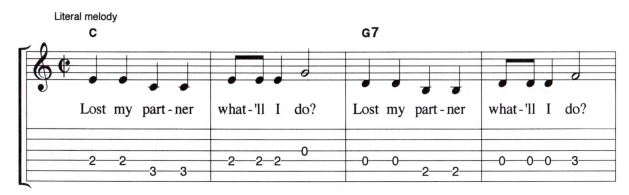

Lost my part-ner what-'ll I do? Lost my part-ner what-'ll I do?

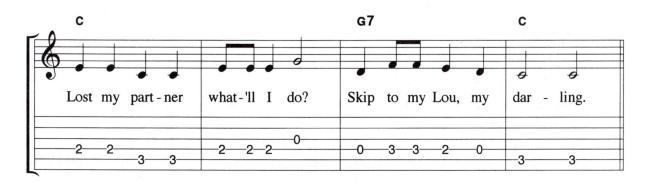

Lost my part-ner what-'ll I do? Skip to my Lou, my dar – ling.

Skeleton melody with strums

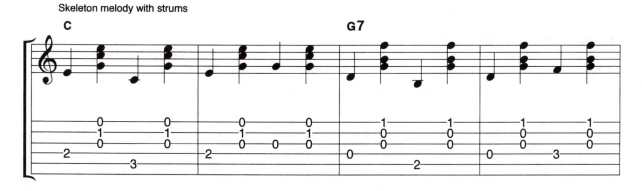

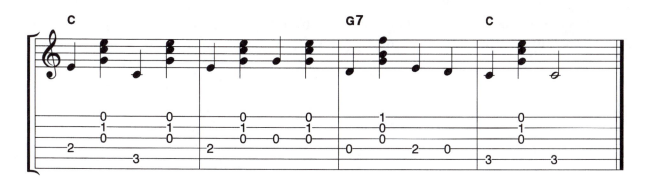

CREATIVE WORK. Add hammers to "Skip to My Lou." Then try it with the bump-diddy beat, both with and without hammers.

MORE CREATIVE WORK. Sing this song with a bass-brush accompaniment, using bass runs.

Track 45: Ear Training–Skip to My Lou

Here's some street learning. Listen to it, try to hear what's going on, and try to incorporate elements of what you hear into your own playing. Do your best. Your goal is not necessarily to play exactly what I'm playing. It's to get some ideas from what I'm playing so you can create your own version of the song.

Track 46: Arranging–Mary Had a Little Lamb

More street learning. First, review track 19. Then listen to this track and use what you hear to work toward your own arrangement.

CREATIVE WORK. Don't be too ambitious. Aim for an arrangement that's simpler and more skeletal than what you hear in this track, and add the hammers and extra notes later. Don't be afraid of fumbling around to find the notes you want. The usual process of creating your own arrangement, especially as a novice, is to create a disorganized mess that you only pull together after hours, days, or weeks of experiment. This is normal. You can be working on this arrangement while you proceed to the next tracks.

Breaking the Rules with Bass Notes

Track 47: Accompaniment Version of Cripple Creek

By now, I hope you're used to using alternating-bass-note accompaniments (tracks 10–14). Now that you've also learned about finding other notes in the Carter style, it's time to break the alternating-bass-note rules.

Here's an accompaniment to "Cripple Creek" that works with singing, but that I'd use especially if I were backing up another solo instrument like a fiddle or banjo. To my taste, it supports the melody line nicely, sometimes copying it and sometimes not. In order to do this, it breaks the rules of alternation, often by incorporating Carter-style thinking. It even dares to use repeated, nonalternating notes.

TRACK 47. ACCOMPANIMENT VERSION OF CRIPPLE CREEK

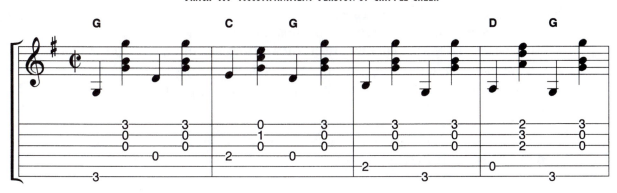

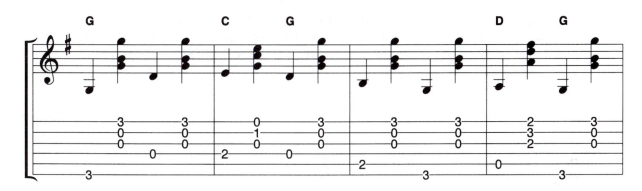

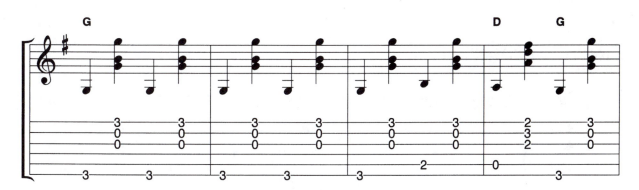

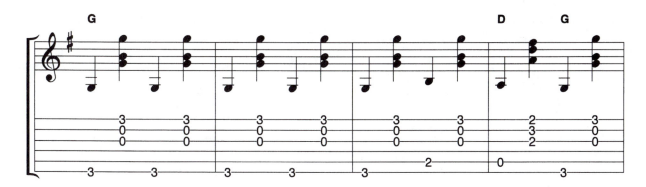

CREATIVE WORK. You'll notice that this accompaniment doesn't call for demanding technique. It calls for something even greater: you've got to think and experiment and reach your own conclusions. This is harder than copying someone else's arrangement.

Go back and rethink all the songs you know in terms of this track. Work at it on and off, at your pleasure, for the rest of your life. Meanwhile, keep working on the preceding tracks until you are comfortable and are ready to go on to a new style starting with track 48 in the next chapter.

Conclusion to Carter-Style Playing

You've only had a taste of the Carter style, but a memorable one, I hope. Complications arise when the songs themselves become more difficult, especially in keys other than C and G, requiring more left-hand acrobatics. But all the principles of the Carter style are here.

Chapter 11 provides several more Carter-style arrangements (tracks 70–73). You're ready to go there now, if you wish.

Melodic Fingerpicking

Preparation for Melodic Fingerpicking

In the Carter style, you play a melody in the bass and accompany it by strumming the high notes of the chords in between melody notes.

Melodic fingerpicking is just about the opposite. In fingerpicking, you play the melody on the high strings while you keep up a fast, steady alternating-bass accompaniment with your thumb on the low strings. The repeating bass strings keep the rhythm and chord sound going constantly.

As with Carter-style playing, some songs work better than others in this style and in a given key. You learn from experience.

Before going further, review pattern picking (tracks 31–34). This will get your fingers in shape to begin melodic fingerpicking. It's also important that the standard alternating bass patterns (chapter 5) be second nature to you by now. If not, review them, so that you have no hesitation in knowing which alternating bass notes to use for a given chord.

Also review your G-chord fingering. In order to play in this style, you absolutely *must* be using the G-chord fingering shown in the chord chart in figure 2.1, using fingers 2,3,4, with your index finger free (as if ready to go to G7).

LISTENING. The great finger stylists of traditional American music continue to be an inspiration for contemporary guitarists. Modern finger-style playing is often more complex, but never more elegant, than the work of the older generation of players.

I've already mentioned in track 21 the traditional Etta Baker and the more contemporary player Taj Mahal.

Mississippi John Hurt continues to be the inspiration for the thumpy, brushy picking sound you'll learn a few tracks from now. Listen to *Avalon Blues* (Rounder), among his many CDs.

Doc Watson is equally facile as a flat-picker and fingerpicker. His early, predominantly solo, albums like *Doc Watson* and *Best of Doc Watson, 1964–1968* (Vanguard) show off his playing to maximum advantage. The *Best of . . .* album includes "Doc's Guitar," which relies on picking that's roughly a cross between what you learned in track 33 and what you're going to learn in the coming tracks.

Blind Blake's recordings of the 1920s are virtuosic and have inspired many modern hot-shot pickers. Listen to *Best of Blind Blake* (Yazoo/Shanachie).

Elizabeth Cotten's graceful left-handed style documents the transition from nineteenth-century parlor guitar to African-American fingerpicking (e.g., *Freight Train*, Smithsonian Folkways). That style comes to fruition in the playing of John Jackson (*Blues and Country Dance Tunes from Virginia*, Arhoolie.)

Traditional country music fingerpicking reached one of its high points in the busy, jazz-influenced style of Merle Travis (*Walkin' the Strings*, Capitol). Travis influenced Doc Watson, Chet Atkins, and almost everyone else who followed.

Listen to the great finger pickers of the past and present, and you'll hear a variety of distinct, personal styles. All of their styles start with the basic fingerpicking gestures and rhythms you'll be learning in the coming tracks. Then they go beyond, each in their own way.

Track 48: Simple Pinch Pattern

As with Carter-style playing, always keep your complete chord shape in place as much as possible. Now, just pinch on the first and third bass notes of every four. Get the feeling of this move firmly in your fingers. Pretty soon you're going to use those pinched high notes to eke out melodies, so the gesture needs to become second nature. Keep the thumb steady, and use your index finger for the pinch.

As you begin to play this pattern, you'll find it natural to accent the beats that come with the pinches. This is a good way to approach most contemporary singer-songwriter songs. For older-sounding material in a rural-style, with a more authentic bounce, shift the emphasis to thumb strokes two and four instead. This shifting of the accent off the normal beat is called *syncopation*.

Listen for the syncopation as the track shifts from a straight to a syncopated beat. Notice how the heavy strokes are so heavy that my thumb even brushes down across the next string. This shift in accent is what gives fingerpicking its essential liveliness. A lot of players don't depend on the thumb muscles alone but incorporate a little wrist movement that adds some of the weight of the hand to the stroke.

Remember, syncopating is not necessarily better than not syncopating. It's a matter of choice. Some guitarists favor one beat over another as a matter of personal style. Others vary it according to the feeling of the song.

Track 48. Simple Pinch Pattern

CREATIVE WORK. Practice chords and chord progressions of your choice until you're comfortable keeping this picking pattern steady, even across chord changes in which you have to change the alternating bass strings. It shouldn't take long. Go on the next track as soon as you feel even moderately comfortable with this one.

Track 49: Pinching on Different Strings

Now try pinching on different strings. Some people prefer doing all their pinching with the index finger, letting it move among the three high strings. Others prefer to distribute the work among several fingers—for example, second finger on the first string, but index finger on the third and second strings. Not many choose to use all three picking fingers.

It's easiest to just stick with your index finger for now. But if you're inclined to do otherwise, it's okay to do what comes naturally.

TRACK 49. PINCHING ON DIFFERENT STRINGS

CREATIVE WORK. Get used to playing various notes of your own choice across the three high strings. If you're having trouble working across the chord progression, then just experiment with one chord at a time for starters. Work with various chords and chord progressions of your choice.

Track 50: Pinching Extra Notes

In Carter-style playing, you sometimes have to alter chord shapes to get melody notes that aren't part of the actual chord fingering. The same thing goes for fingerpicking. Just lift up or add a finger as necessary in order to get in the melody note while keeping the chord shape in place as much as possible. In most cases, the added finger is going to be the pinky because the pinky is the finger most likely to be free. In this track, the third-fret notes added to the C chord (measure 1), the G chord (measure 4), and the F chord (measure 6) are all pinky notes.

In this and some later tracks, you'll encounter melodies that require altered fingerings like those in figure 9.1. Play around with these shapes right now to get used to them. Then work on the music from the track.

FIGURE 9.1. ALTERED FINGERINGS

Shapes Based on C

Shapes Based on G and G7

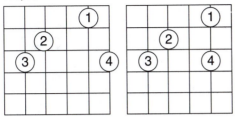

TRACK 50. PINCHING EXTRA NOTES

CREATIVE WORK. Experiment with this idea, using different chords and progressions. Don't be afraid of playing wrong notes. How else are you going to find out they're wrong?

Playing Melodies

Track 51: Skip to My Lou, Fingerpicked with Pinches

Review track 44.

Track 51 presents two versions of "Skip to My Lou," played consecutively. The first is the literal melody, filled with pinches. It may be accurate, but notice how singsongy it sounds compared with the second, more economical version. Once again, less is more. To my taste, the second version is more engaging and listenable.

TRACK 51. SKIP TO MY LOU, FINGERPICKED WITH PINCHES

Almost literal melody

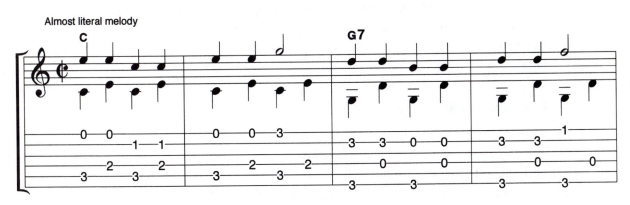

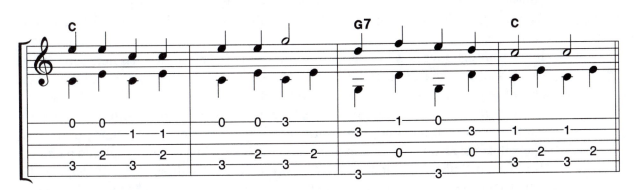

Skeleton melody with varied pinching

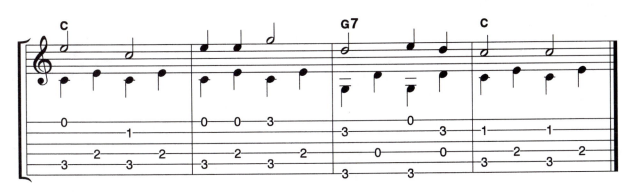

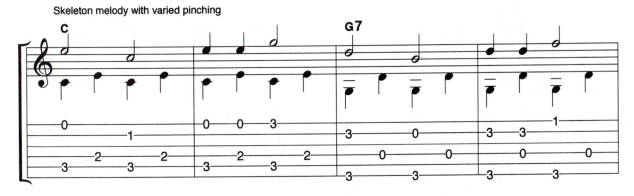

CREATIVE WORK. Try to flesh out the second version by incorporating some of the repeated notes found in the first version. Perhaps you can find some balance between the two versions that pleases you. One way to approach this exercise is to work from the first version and start cutting notes—just not as many as I cut to get to my second version. Don't be afraid of mistakes and irregularities. They're part of the learning process.

Track 52: Railroad Bill, Fingerpicked Version

Review track 21.

Now at last you graduate from nursery rhymes to real songs. And if you haven't yet heard the wonderful versions of "Railroad Bill" recorded by Etta Baker and Taj Mahal mentioned in track 21, now would be a good time. In this track and track 55, you'll take a few steps toward achieving their mastery of fingerpicking style.

As usual, the fast chord changes can be tricky: the C-to-G7 in measure 3 and the F-to-G in measure 10.

In measure 3, notice how I've broken the rules and used 5,4 as my bass notes on the fast G7. This makes it easier to keep the picking stable, because strings 5,4 are also the bass strings for the surrounding C chords. Better yet, it also sounds good.

In measure 10, isolate the chord change. Practice going from an F chord to an altered G shape that has your pinky coming right down on the second string, third fret. You don't need to put any finger at all on the first string, because the first string doesn't get played here.

The track includes both slow and *at tempo* versions of "Railroad Bill." *At tempo* is the term musicians use to describe the normal performing tempo of a piece that they've been rehearsing more slowly. The at tempo versions also contain a little more syncopation, with added emphasis on the second and third out of every four bass notes. Along with this emphasis comes a heavier, broader thumb stroke that tends to brush onto the next higher string as well. Anyone learning to fingerpick has to choose between cultivating clean or brushy thumb strokes.

LISTENING. The great master of brushy thumb strokes in fingerpicking was Mississippi John Hurt. His bass notes rise up out of the texture of his picking like champagne bubbles, giving a lift to his entire sound. Etta Baker, on the other hand, generally played with cleaner strokes.

Track 52. Railroad Bill, Fingerpicked Version

Track 53: Syncopated Pinching

Now let's take pinching a step further by changing the placement of the second high note. Instead of playing it as a pinch, you'll move it into the space between the third and fourth thumb strokes. Moving the melody note off the thumb beat like this is an even more dramatic form of syncopation. Listen to how much bounce and drive it adds to the picking pattern.

TRACK 53. SYNCOPATED PINCHING

CREATIVE WORK. In this example, the high notes are all on the first string. Try playing the same rhythm with the high notes on the second and third strings instead. Then go back and forth among all three strings. Experiment at first with one chord, then with different chords and progressions.

MORE CREATIVE WORK. Practice going back and forth between the syncopated and plain (track 48) versions of this pattern until you can change between them at will. Practice at first on single chords, then on chord changes and progressions.

Track 54: Skip to My Lou, Syncopated

This version of "Skip to My Lou" is based on the same skeleton melody as used on track 51. Notice how much more lively and interesting it sounds here. But even the syncopated beat can get boring through repetition, so I played the last G7 measure with straight pinches to add some variety.

TRACK 54. SKIP TO MY LOU, SYNCOPATED

CREATIVE WORK. Work out your own arrangement of this song, varying syncopated and un-syncopated picking.

Track 55: Railroad Bill, Syncopated

This track phrases "Railroad Bill" with syncopated picking. Bill's a troublemaker, and he deserves to get shaken up a little.

That fast C-to-G7 change in measure 3 may throw you a little with the syncopated phrasing; if it does, pull it out and practice it as a separate exercise. The same is true for the fast F-to-G chord change in measure 10. You need to be absolutely secure about your left-hand moves in this spot in order for this passage not to sound jerky. As before, work on making the fast F-to-G change by dropping your pinky onto the second string, third fret as you get out of F and into G.

TRACK 55. RAILROAD BILL, SYNCOPATED

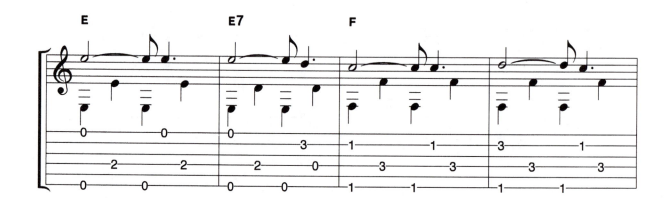

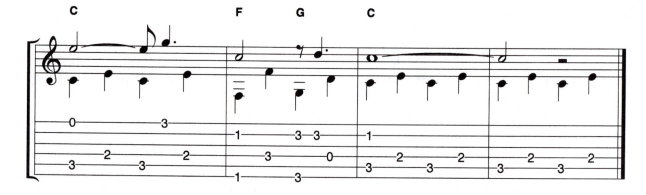

CREATIVE WORK. Try to create your own version of "Railroad Bill" in which some measures use the syncopated pattern as demonstrated here, while others use the completed pinched, on-the-beat pattern. Your ultimate goal, one to always strive for, is to be able to place your melody notes either pinched directly on the beat, or syncopated between thumb notes, freely according to your own will. Again—and I can never say this enough—you must accept stops and starts, roughness and imperfections, while you work this out.

Track 56: Mary Had a Little Lamb, Fingerpicked with Pinches

Back to nursery rhymes again. But that only means that I'm going to ask you to do something difficult on your own. For the time being, however, let's just get the melody of this song under control. Play it with pinches as written, and make sure that you're completely secure with it before moving on to the next track.

Track 56. Mary Had a Little Lamb, Fingerpicked with Pinches

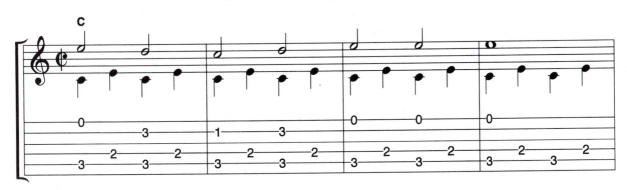

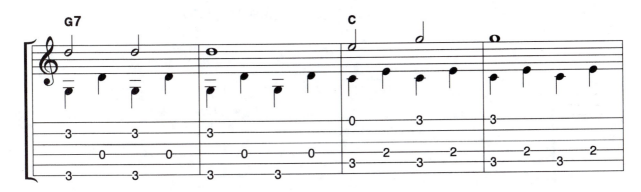

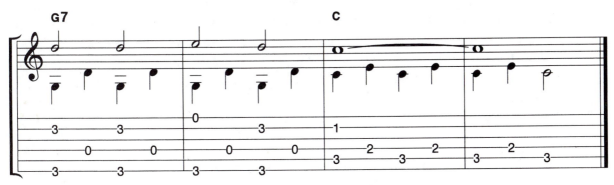

Track 57: Mary Had a Little Lamb, with Syncopated Melody

Now it's time to take off the training wheels. Here's the start of "Mary Had a Little Lamb," and it's up to you to finish it on your own. If you're having trouble, remember the basic principle of problem solving: Break down the problem into solvable parts. That means not dealing with more than one thing at a time. If you're still not absolutely comfortable with the simple, pinched melody as given in the preceding track, or with the picking pattern as given in track 53, then you're not ready to tackle this track yet.

You may also consider tackling the song one measure or one phrase at a time and then work a little later on assembling the parts you've rehearsed separately. Many creative musicians like to work out songs by combining these two processes. Work on measures or phrases, trying to get them perfect. In between doing that, work on playing the whole song, however imperfectly, to try to get a handle on its flow. Then work on getting these two processes to fall together.

TRACK 57. MARY HAD A LITTLE LAMB, WITH SYNCOPATED MELODY

CREATIVE WORK. Once you've worked out your syncopated version of "Mary Had a Little Lamb," do what you did in your creative work for "Skip to My Lou" and "Railroad Bill." Make up your own arrangement, combining pinched and syncopated phrasing.

Conclusion to Melodic Fingerpicking

This chapter came in like a lion, but it's going out like a lamb. We learned the rudiments of phrasing: how to phrase notes on or off the thumb beat at your will. Singers are allowed to phrase a melody as freely as their style of music permits, and there's no reason why guitarists shouldn't strive for the same freedom. We've begun along the path of freedom, while still keeping the left hand simple.

Country Blues

The Blues Sound

The blues is a feeling, they say. The blues comes out of your soul, they say. The blues ain't nothin' but a good man (or woman) feelin' bad.

Well, this may all be true, but you'll just have to excuse me if I'm reluctant to try to teach you how to feel. What I can teach you are some of the musical and structural characteristics of the blues.

Begin by strumming the following chord progression. Run through it for at least a minute, until you get it into your ears:

A A D D A A D D

Now try this:

A7 A7 D7 D7 A7 A7 D7 D7

What's the difference? The version with the sevenths sounds bluesy, right? Inference: Seventh chords sound bluesy. Like many casual inferences, however, this one isn't logically correct. In fact, seventh chords only sound bluesy depending on their context: how they fit with other chords. This is a case where they sound bluesy. Try going back and forth between a plain E and a B7 chord, and you'll notice that the B7 doesn't sound that bluesy.

The chords A7 and D7 in the previous progression sound bluesy because the added sevenths are *blue notes*. These notes, which are characteristic of African-American music, don't belong to the plain vanilla do-re-mi scale of nursery songs and Mozart. Think of them as extra colors that add excitement.

Blue notes are found in the seventh chord of the key you're playing in (an E7 chord in the key of E) and the seventh chord four letters above that (an A7 chord in the key of E). If this sounds confusing, don't worry about explanations. Practically, the solution is easy. Just use a lot of seventh chords.

In the next section, you're going to learn your first blues song.

The Blues Form: Twelve-Bar Blues

The twelve-bar blues is the most typical blues form. Not all blues are twelve-bar blues. There are some other more or less standard forms as well, in addition to a hodgepodge of songs that people call blues merely because they sound and feel bluesy. Which is good enough.

But twelve-bar blues is what people generally think of, even if they don't know the technical term, when you mention the word *blues*. It's what another musician will start playing if you say, "Let's play some blues." It's a form that everyone who plays the blues learns to feel instinctively and unerringly. How do you do this? By playing and listening to a lot of blues.

The 12-bar blues consists of three sung lines.
First you sing a line: *Hello blues, blues how do you do?*
Then repeat it, maybe varied: *Hello blues, say blues how do you do?*
Then you sing a new line: *I'm doing real fine, good morning, how are you?*

This is the poetic structure of the blues. The verse form is AAB. Now let's look at the musical form.

Bar is another word for measure, which in blues means a unit of four beats (four foot taps). Each sung line typically gets four measures, totaling twelve for a three-line verse—therefore, twelve-bar blues. Using the standard twelve-bar blues chord changes, the timing works out as follows. Strum it out on your guitar, playing *four beats* on each chord that's written:

E   A* E E
A   A   E E
B7 A   E E

Now let's pick up on the lesson you learned about blue notes and strum the same chord progression with seventh chords instead. Sure enough, it sounds bluesier:

E7 A7 E7 E7
A7 A7 E7 E7
B7 A7 E7 E7

---

*About half of all twelve-bar blues go to the A chord (or equivalent chord in a different key) at this point. The other half use the E chord all the way through the first line. It's not random—a given blues song goes either one way or the other.

Now try strumming through the following version, combining regular and seventh chords to vary the sound of the progression. This is very typical.

E   A7 E E7

A   A7 E E7

B7 A7 E E7

If you'd like to hear a recorded version of this chord pattern, listen to track 58, where I strum through the progression once in the key of G before I start singing. Transposed to G, it goes like this:

G   C7 G G7

C   C7 G G7

D7 C7 G G7

Transposing the Blues

As you work out more advanced ways of playing the blues, you'll be sticking to the keys of E and G here. The keys of A, C, and D are also used. Each has its own special character. Get used to strumming the blues form in all these keys as well—four beats for each written chord, just as you've been doing it.

KEY OF A

A   D7 A A7

D   D7 A A7

E7 D7 A A7

KEY OF C (WHERE MANY GUITARISTS LAZILY CHOOSE TO USE F RATHER THAN F7)

C   F C C7

F   F C C7

G7 F C C7

KEY OF D

D   G7 D D7

G   G7 D D7

A7 G7 D D7

CREATIVE WORK. Get thoroughly used to the chord changes for twelve-bar blues. Pay most attention to the keys of E and G because they're the ones you'll be using later.

These chord changes need to become absolutely second nature if you're going to become an accomplished blues player. Continue to play around with going back and forth between regular and seventh chords in places other than those written out in the previous examples.

In the early days of the blues, more often than today, some rural stylists deliberately varied the twelve-bar structure. They knew what they were doing and created their own formal variations. Others played loosely, varying the structure at random; mostly they were soloists, who didn't have to worry about keeping the music together with other players.

The great Lightnin' Hopkins (see the following listening section) was such a performer. He often skipped or added beats. One reason he did so was because his mind was elsewhere; he was improvising his lyrics as he went along and sometimes needed to strum a little to give himself time to think. At his best, Lightnin' Hopkins was a great singer and a brilliant composer of blues lyrics.

You probably don't have this excuse. It's more important to be strict. That way you can have fun playing with other guitarists. No one will want to play with you if you don't know how to make the chord changes in the right place.

LISTENING. There are so many great country blues stylists that I can't begin to offer a fair or historical discography. I'll offer a useful one instead; one that pertains to the styles you'll be studying here.

The great master of the thumping, syncopated style you'll work on starting with track 59 was Josh White. You have to be careful with Josh White CDs because later in life he became a member of the urban folk-song movement in New York and recorded a certain amount of nonblues material that was not too good. Listen to albums like *Blues Singer* (Legacy) or *Free and Equal Blues* (Smithsonian Folkways). He often departed from the simple strum we do in this book, but listen for his grace and fluency.

Another master of the thumping strum, with a very different take on it, was John Lee Hooker. Listen for his driving boogie rhythms especially on earlier work like *The Very Best of John Lee Hooker* (Rhino). Hooker also added pinching patterns to his strum, something you will learn starting with track 66. A completely different stylist who also relied a great deal on pinching (track 66) and triplet (track 67) rhythms was Robert Johnson (*King of the Delta Blues Singers*, Columbia).

Big Bill Broonzy was another great singer and guitarist, one who developed the kind of right-hand freedom aimed for in track 69. Broonzy is nowadays best known for his piece "Hey Hey Baby," which Eric Clapton popularized. Broonzy worked in several styles during his long and varied career; for our purposes, listen to *Trouble in Mind* (Smithsonian Folkways).

Lightnin' Hopkins relied greatly on pinching and triplets. His seemingly simple but rhythmically dynamic guitar style was a foil for great overall performances. At his best (*The Gold Star Sessions*, Arhoolie), Hopkins is unsurpassed for depth of feeling and soulfulness.

You'll discover that the main feature of country blues guitar playing is keeping a steady bass going while you play high notes against it. The following section is devoted to nothing more than learning some of the basic right-hand moves needed to get this sound. Lightnin' Hopkins is not a great model for absolutely steady bass notes (not that it matters in a player of such feeling). Two influential guitarists who are good models for this technique are Mance Lipscomb (*Texas Songster*, Arhoolie) and Bonnie Raitt's master, Mississippi Fred MacDowell (*You Gotta Move*, Arhoolie).

Blues Tracks

Track 58: Hello Blues, Strummed and Sung

Now try singing a real blues. This one, "Hello Blues," consists of verses from folk tradition, which in one form or another have made their way into many different blues songs by various performers.

You're entitled to wonder, at this point, why I've spent so much time asking you to pound out blues chords, four beats at a time, without getting into a song.

The answer is this: The blues structure is an abstraction. It exists independent of the lyrics. Different sung lines may be longer or shorter. They may start on the foot tap or between taps. The sung syllables may be spread out or be accented in all kinds of different ways. But no matter how differently the words may fall against the chords, the chord structure of the blues is absolute.

In addition, you'll notice on this track that there are a good seven or eight beats between lines. This is the space where a good guitarist puts in a little melodic figure, understandably called a *fill*, to fill out the line. No one does this more deliciously than B. B. King, accompanying himself. You'll be using a very simple fill when you arrange this song for guitar in track 64. In the meantime, notice how I cleverly change to seventh chords to help fill out that space at the end of the line. (Well, it's not that clever. Blues guitarists and pianists have been doing it since the blues began.) Remember, give each chord four beats.

```
G           C7              G       G7
Hello blues, blues how do you do?
C           C7              G       G7
Hello blues, say blues how do you do?
    D               C7              G       G7
I'm doing real fine, good morning, how are you?
```

Got up this morning, blues all 'round my bed,
Got up this morning with the blues all 'round my bed,
Blues in my coffee, blues all in my bread.

Lay down last night, tried to take my rest,
Lay down to sleep last night, and I tried to take my rest,
But my mind kept ramblin' like the wild geese in the west.

CREATIVE WORK. Strum and sing this song in the keys of E, A, C, and D. (If you find that some of these keys are too high or low for voice, just wait for everyone to leave the house and then sing them.)

Track 59: The Thumping Blues Strum

The picking pattern I call the thumping blues strum works best if you start on the upstroke. It's syncopated with an accented upstroke. You'll find it easier to get into the syncopated groove if you start with the accented upstroke, counting with a strong "and" the way I do on the track. Swipe up with your index finger across three strings. (In real life, guitarists will swipe one, two, or three strings depending on the sound they want. Let's go for three.) It's a tough move. To put maximum power into it, pull up a little with the entire hand instead of just using finger strength.

In between upstrokes, right on the foot tap, the thumb plays the same bass note over and over like a steady beat on a bass drum. Some of the old blues masters (listen to Mance Lipscomb) play the bass note cleanly. Others (e.g., Big Bill Broonzy's solo work from the 1950s) play with a strong, broad brushy stroke that takes in two or three of the bass strings in one swoop. The effect is powerful.

Coupled with the thumb stroke is a muting, or dampening (some people call it damping), of the strings right after the thumb stroke. This is what creates the thumping, percussive effect. Don't propel your thumb from the base of the joint alone. Move your whole wrist. As you make the thumb stroke, rotate your wrist and twist your hand a little so that the side of your hand above the pinky comes to rest on the strings, silencing them decisively and even a bit brutally. The thumb stroke and the wrist dampening action come in one smooth move with no pause between them.

As with the thumb stroke, different guitarists handle the dampening gesture differently. Some deaden the strings so quickly that all you hear is a drumlike thump. Others let the note ring a little.

At the same time as the mute, many guitarists will also release left-hand pressure on the strings. This action silences the fretted strings with the left hand, reinforcing the dampening motion of the right hand.

This strum involves the whole body to some degree. It should be hard and powerful. Many guitarists who do this move prefer to wear finger picks. If you use bare fingers, don't practice too intensely for long periods until you build up some right-hand calluses.

Because this strum starts on the upstroke, simultaneously with the upbeat portion of the foot tap, it causes the entire piece to be felt ahead of the beat. This propulsive feeling is an essential ingredient in the sound of many styles of African-American music.

In addition, I'm playing this pattern on the track with a swing feel, which means that the notes are not equal. Listen carefully, and you'll hear that the thumb stroke, including the silenced space of the mute, is longer than the upstroke. In fact, the upstroke takes up one-third of the beat, while the thumb stroke takes up two-thirds. It's easier to get the feeling into your body by listening and playing along with the track than it is to think about it.

As you listen to blues guitarists, you'll find that they play with more or less of a swing feel depending on the mood of the piece or on their own personal styles.

As with fingerpicking, continue to form complete chord shapes with your left hand even if all the notes from the chord aren't being used.

Track 59. The Thumping Blues Strum

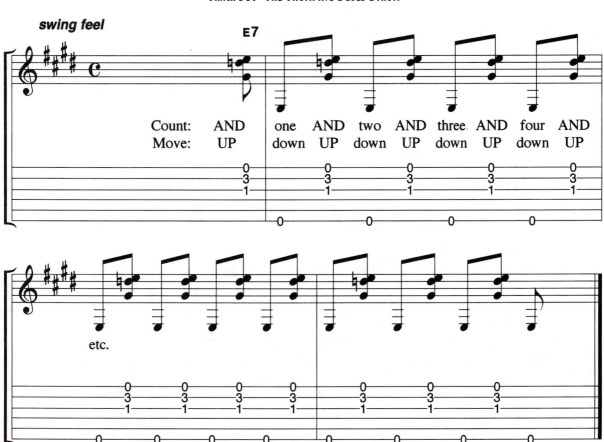

CREATIVE WORK. Practice this strum with individual chords until you feel it getting smooth, comfortable, and flowing. It may take a while to master the muting. Then try the strum on chord progressions, always remembering to thump on the appropriate bass note for each chord.

Track 60: Thumping Melody Notes

In the last example, the music notation and tablature showed all three of the notes caught by the upstroke. In this example and in most of the examples from now on, I'm going to make the music easier to read by only showing the one note to start the upstroke on. Please continue to play that note with a broad swipe that actually takes in two or three strings, and let the high notes ring out until they get muted as part of the following thumb stroke.

Here, you're going to play some melody notes with the strum. It's similar to fingerpicking. Just add extra melody notes to the chord with a free finger (which will usually be the pinky). The dissonance that comes with the E chord in this track is an important ingredient in the blues. Don't be afraid of it. Jimi Hendrix wasn't.

Get used to these altered E7 and A7 shapes a little before you work on the track (figure 10.1). Yes, the E7 is supposed to sound that dissonant. It's a blue note. Go back and forth between these shapes and regular E7 and A7 shapes.

FIGURE 10.1. ALTERED E7 AND A7 SHAPES

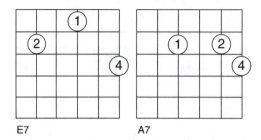

E7   A7

In track 60, notice how the accented upstroke pulls you into making the chord change on the upstroke, ahead of the foot tap. Don't think about it too hard; just let it happen. It will feel natural once you get in the groove.

TRACK 60. THUMPING MELODY NOTES

CREATIVE WORK. Experiment with adding melody notes to other chords, on the basis of your experience with fingerpicking. Don't worry if the notes you play don't sound too bluesy—the idea is just to continue feeling the strum. *Hint:* To sound more bluesy, try going back and forth between plain and seventh chords.

Also practice going back and forth between any two chords of your choice. Don't even try to add melody notes. Just feel the sense of flow and propulsion that comes from making the chord change on the upstroke. The strumming pattern itself will lead you naturally into doing this. You may find that helps to say *AND one AND two AND three AND four* to help you make the chord change on the *AND* before every *one*.

You can work on these exercises while you go ahead to the next track.

Track 61: Thumping Melody Notes with G and C

This track helps consolidate the technique learned in track 60 and also prepares the way for tracks 63 and 64.

The melody expressed in this track requires you to play a G chord with a pinky melody note on the second string, third fret. From this chord, you go directly to a C chord with a pinky melody note added in the same place, the second string, third fret (figure 10.2).

FIGURE 10.2. MOVING FROM ALTERED G TO ALTERED C WITH THUMPING MELODY NOTES

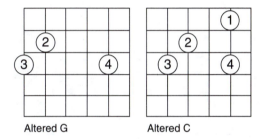

Altered G   Altered C

Before you learn this track, practice going back and forth between these two chords *while keeping your pinky in place.*

TRACK 61. THUMPING MELODY NOTES WITH G AND C

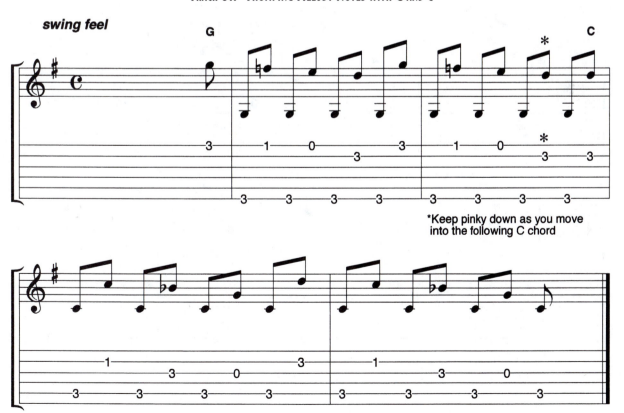

*Keep pinky down as you move into the following C chord

CREATIVE WORK. Play around with the sequence of notes from this track. Play them in different orders. Twist them around. Try to find more notes that sound good (which means not being afraid of finding notes that sound bad.) In this example, the high notes are constantly moving. As you experiment, don't be afraid to play the same note twice or many times in a row.

Track 62: Hello Blues Accompaniment in G

This entire accompaniment is written out, but it really doesn't need to be. All that happens is that you constantly go *UP down UP down UP down UP down,* the *ups* with a brushing index finger and the *downs* with a thumping thumb. The index finger goes back and forth between the third and first strings.

TRACK 62. HELLO BLUES ACCOMPANIMENT IN G

CREATIVE WORK. Try this strum on other chord progressions, including the following. Also include the standard twelve-bar blues progressions in five keys given at the beginning of this chapter.

C   C7   F   C

A   A7   D   Dm

Am Dm Am E7

Track 63: Hello Blues Melody

This track contains the bare vocal melody for "Hello Blues." Learn it now. Finger it by working off chord shapes so that at any given time, your fingers are making as much of the chord shape as possible. As is often the case, the pinky gets the brunt of the work.

TRACK 63. HELLO BLUES MELODY

Notice the wide open spaces at the end of every line. This is where guitar players (and other instrumentalists) play their fills between the sung lines. Part of becoming a blues player is learning to feel this count exactly. It comes with experience. Playing with others hastens the process.

CREATIVE WORK. I play the notes cleanly on the track and count out the fills without playing. Create your own version in which you play the notes with brush strokes so you can hear some of the chord along with the melody note. Then try strumming the chord on the fills instead of just counting them out loud.

Track 64: Hello Blues Solo

Now that you've gotten used to the melody for "Hello Blues," try expressing it with the thumping strum. As usual, remember that the high notes represent the notes on which you start your brushy upstrokes. Catch two or three strings on each stroke.

Notice how the strum, by beginning on the upstroke, automatically puts the melody on the upbeat just ahead of the foot tap. But don't think too hard about it. Feel it from the track, and just let it happen.

Notice also that the fill portion of the solo is very simple—mostly just a repeated G7.

TRACK 64. HELLO BLUES SOLO

CREATIVE WORK. Are you bored by the fill because it's just one note? Well, do something about it! Find some other notes. You know how.

Track 65: Skip to My Blues

Review track 51.

I think you're ready to show your street smarts. Here's the kickoff for "Skip to My Lou," played with the thumping blues strum. The old blues masters played many nonblues songs using blues strums. So can you. Finish it up yourself.

TRACK 65. SKIP TO MY BLUES

Track 66: Pinching the Blues

Review track 48.

As with fingerpicking, the object of blues playing is to be able to place melody notes where and when you want them. So far, you've just been alternating up and down, so the melody notes have always been in between the thumb notes, but never along with them.

Here—this time with all the brushed notes written out completely—is a blues strum with pinches. The pinches let you place melody notes on the same beat as the thumb notes, right along with the foot tap.

TRACK 66. PINCHING THE BLUES

CREATIVE WORK. Play this rhythm on different chords of your choice. Try upstroking at different times from the first, second, and third strings. Then go on the practice with chord progressions of your choice, including the standard twelve-bar blues progressions in five keys given at the beginning of this chapter.

Track 67: Pinching the Blues with Triplets

Another important rhythm in blues style is the *triplet*. Triplets, as we use them here, are three notes played evenly in the space of one beat. Play them using three quick upstrokes. The first upstroke comes on the foot tap, so include the bass note played with a pinch. Track 67 alternates a regular swing feel beat with pinched triplets.

In music notation, triplets are written enclosed by a bracket with a little *3*. They're not conventionally marked in tablature, so you need to listen to the example of the track or look at the music notation.

TRACK 67. PINCHING THE BLUES WITH TRIPLETS

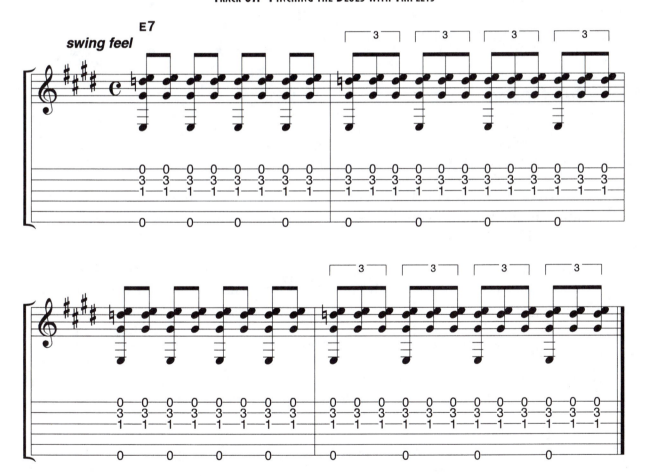

CREATIVE WORK. Play this rhythm on various chords of your choice and then on progressions. Try randomly going back and forth between regular pinches and triplets until you feel comfortably in command of triplet picking and can play them smoothly and at will.

Track 68: Hello Blues Solo with Pinches

Review tracks 63 and 64.

Here's the beginning of a new version of "Hello Blues." Remember that the written music and tablature only indicate the note on which to start your brushy upstroke. As usual, catch another one or two strings in addition to the ones that are written.

All the melody notes are pinched, and everything falls squarely on the foot tap until you get to the fill. Then go into triplets for the last three beats of the fill.

There are two new things to learn in this track: pinching a melody and playing the triplet rhythm in the fill. You may find it useful to practice them separately, one measure or a few measures at a time, before you try to combine them.

TRACK 68. HELLO BLUES SOLO WITH PINCHES

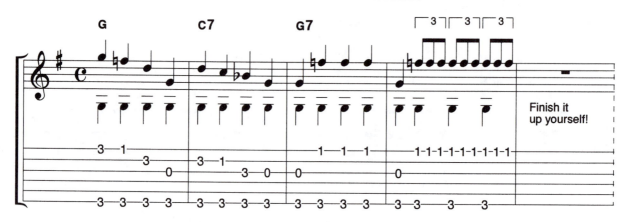

CREATIVE WORK. Play around with the melody. Try to play the fill differently. Vary the rhythm of the fill. In my version, one pinched beat is followed by three beats of triplets. Come up with some other combinations of single pinches and triplets. Change the notes of the fill.

MORE CREATIVE WORK. Review track 61 and see if it gives you any new ideas for working on this track. *Hint:* There's an extra melody note in track 61 that doesn't appear in this track. Maybe you can work it in.

Track 69: Blues in E

The key of E, when you play in it at its full potential, is the deepest, darkest, most soulful key for blues playing. You can only scratch the surface with what you know so far, but at least you can scratch it in an interesting way.

This solo does in a simpler way what blues masters like Robert Johnson and Big Bill Broonzy were masters of. It's free, not tied down to a single set of strumming or picking gestures. It goes back and forth among up-down thumping strums, pinches, and triplets. At the same time, I've kept the left hand simple so you can concentrate on the right.

When you learn to play this piece with fluency, you've come a long way toward understanding country blues and mastering the rhythms of the right hand. You can be as simple or as complicated as you want to in the left hand, but unless you master the right, your playing won't have the blues feeling.

Track 69. Blues in E

CREATIVE WORK. Review the thumped and pinched versions of "Hello Blues" (tracks 64 and 68). Try to work out a version—or several different versions—of "Hello Blues" that incorporates the same variety of rhythms that this track uses. Be prepared to spend a long time at this. Don't be deterred if things fall apart from time to time. Work in four-measure (one-line) units at a time. Work in small phrases and units if you have to.

Conclusion to the Blues

You still have a lot of work ahead of you to master country blues. Left-hand technique can be much more complicated than anything touched on in this book. You've only played in a few keys, and the variety of brilliant personal styles among the old blues masters is astounding. But once you have the basic blues feeling in your picking hand, you're ready to sail into deeper waters.

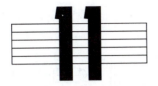

Song Gallery

As a bonus, this chapter includes another nine songs that use the techniques you've learned.

Track 70: Crawdad Song, Carter Style

Review tracks 24 and 36.

   This version of "Crawdad Song" is in Carter style. Notice how, in spaces between sung lines where there are no real melody notes, the bass notes I use are simply the ordinary alternating bass notes for the chord.

   Sometimes, if you choose melody notes over strumming, you can just forget about fingering the chord shape. Especially if the sequence of notes doesn't relate to a chord shape. This is what happens in the F measures.

TRACK 70. CRAWDAD SONG, CARTER STYLE

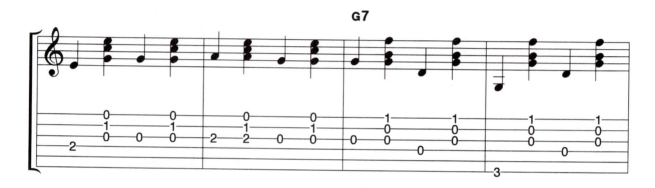

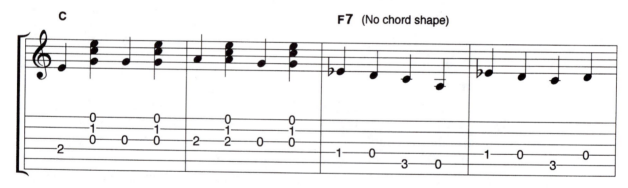

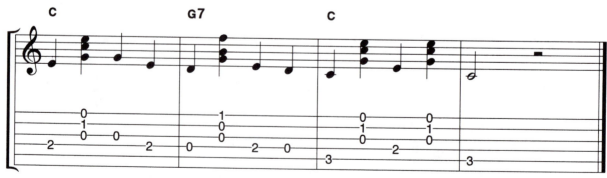

CREATIVE WORK. Add hammers (listen to the recorded track). Use the bump-diddy beat. Can you find places where you'd like to give up some brush strokes and play more melody notes instead?

Track 71: On Top of Old Smoky, Carter Style

Review tracks 25 and 40.

This is a straightforward arrangement. Get it down pat so you can do some creative work with it.

TRACK 71. ON TOP OF OLD SMOKY, CARTER STYLE

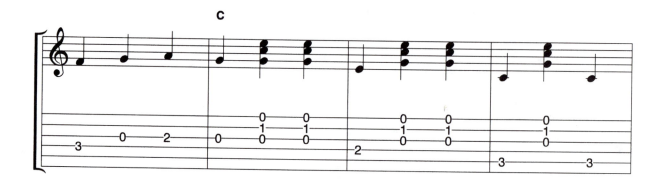

CREATIVE WORK. Try playing the melody with some hammered notes. Try using the bump-diddy rhythm, but not necessarily at every opportunity (listen to the second time through on the track.)

Track 72: This Little Light of Mine, Carter Style

Here is another easy and straightforward arrangement that illustrates how the Carter style works.

Track 72. This Little Light of Mine, Carter Style

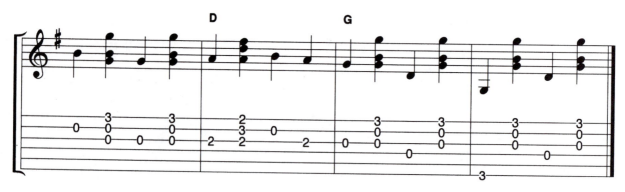

CREATIVE WORK. Try hammers and bump-diddies and see how you like them. This song is so simple I prefer it plain. Sometimes the simpler the song, the simpler its arrangement can be.

Track 73: Railroad Bill, Carter Style

Review tracks 21, 52, and 55.

The melody note with the G7 chord in measure three may give you trouble. I use my pinky and keep the bass notes from the G chord in place. You may prefer to use either your third finger or pinky and not play the G chord bass notes. That would be fine.

TRACK 73. RAILROAD BILL, CARTER STYLE

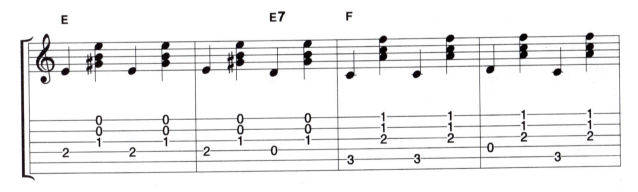

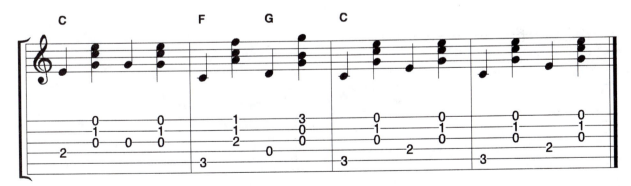

CREATIVE WORK.   As usual, try hammers and bump-diddies. This is another song I like to keep simple. The melody's unusual and stands well by itself.

Track 74: Hello Blues, Fingerpicked

Review tracks 53 and 64.

   Some blues melodies work well melodically fingerpicked with alternating bass notes. "Hello Blues" is certainly one.

TRACK 74. HELLO BLUES, FINGERPICKED

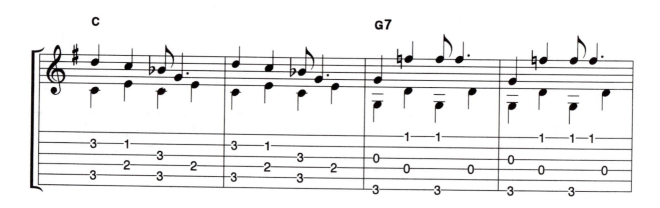

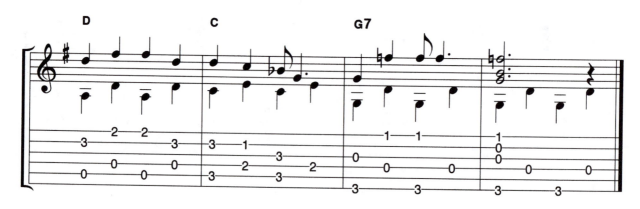

CREATIVE WORK. Notice how, in the D chord measure, all the notes get pinched. This sounds good, brings out the melody line, and helps break up the repeated syncopated rhythm that occurs in all other measures.

Rework this solo to vary the straight pinched rhythms with the syncopated rhythms more freely.

Track 75: Crawdad Song, Fingerpicked

Review tracks 24, 36, and 70.

It's okay to take some liberties with the literal vocal melody when you play an instrumental solo. In fact, there's an art to it. This version doesn't stray far, but it gives you an idea of what begins to be possible.

You learn how to play instrumental variations of sung melodies by listening to the instrumental solos and interludes that often come about two-thirds of the way through a song, and studying the way musicians vary the melody. (Of course, sometimes they choose not to refer to the melody at all, but to play something completely different.)

TRACK 75. CRAWDAD SONG, FINGERPICKED

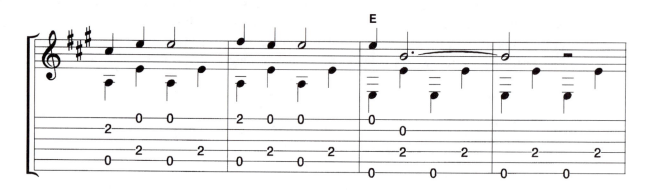

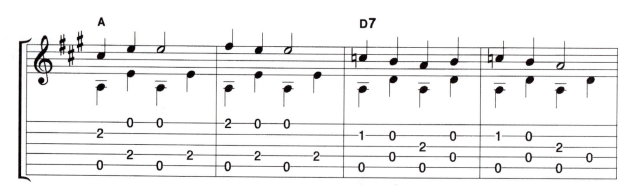

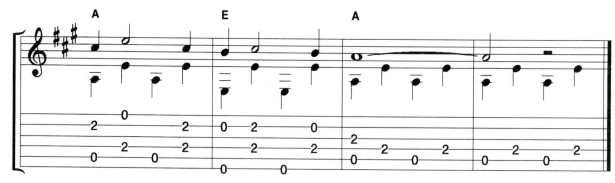

CREATIVE WORK. Try syncopating the phrasing of this version a little more. (Review track 53.) *Hint:* Leave out some melody notes, making the melody even more skeletal. That creates the space you need to move the remaining notes around.

Track 76: This Little Light of Mine, Fingerpicked

Review tracks 22, 60, and 72.

This alternating-bass arrangement incorporates blue notes from the thumping strum exercise in track 60. It's a good example of making a song sound more bluesy by using blue notes that are close to, but not exactly, the melody notes.

TRACK 76. THIS LITTLE LIGHT OF MINE, FINGERPICKED

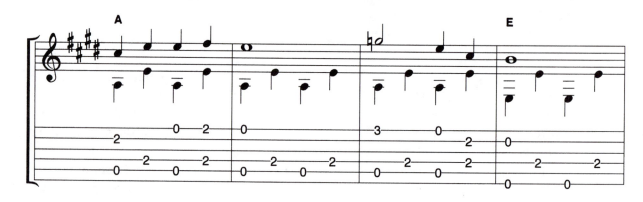

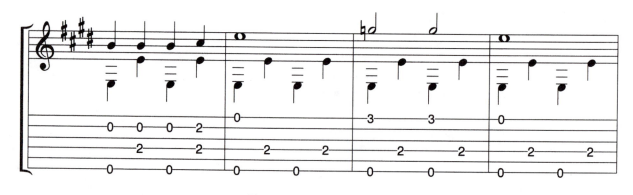

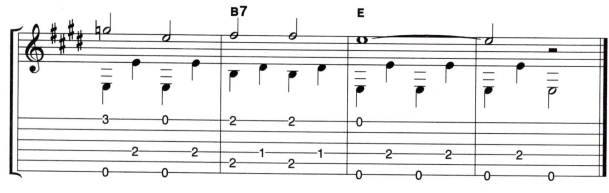

CREATIVE WORK. There are a number of places in this arrangement where you could enhance the blues feeling by changing the chord color from E to E7. Do it.

MORE CREATIVE WORK. Rework this arrangement with the thumping blues strum, using a steady bass. Try it pinched, try it phrased with accented upstrokes, and try it with both these styles combined.

Track 77: Generic Rag

Review track 33.

Whether you call it "Rag Mama," "Salty Dog," "Don't Let Your Deal Go Down," or any of a dozen other names, this chord progression is a standard in ragtime blues and old-time music. People are still writing new words to this chord progression. Strum or pick through the progression by itself a few times to get its feel, four beats per chord.

A7 D7 G7 C

The example in this track uses the chord progression twice through. Each go-through takes eight measures.

In the first eight measures, the melody is expressed with a syncopated picking pattern plucked with just one finger on the first string. There's just the melody, with accompaniment by the thumb.

In the second eight measures, the melody is expressed using the two-finger pattern you learned as an accompaniment pattern in track 33. This pattern still lets the melody note come out on the first string but adds some extra notes on the second string to flesh out the sound.

TRACK 77. GENERIC RAG

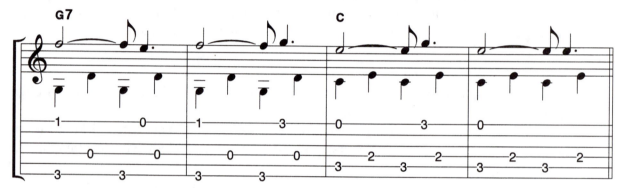

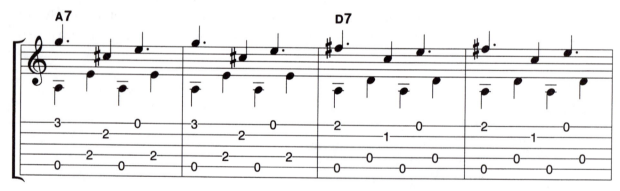

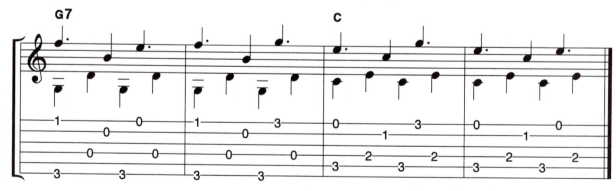